25/-

DISCOURSES ON

KAIVALYOPANIṢAD

Original Upaniṣad Text in Devanāgrī
with Transliteration in Roman letters
and Word - for - Word meaning in Text order

with

Translation

and

Commentary

by

Swami Chinmayananda

CENTRAL CHINMAYA MISSION TRUST
MUMBAI - 400 072.

Printed upto	December	2000	-	20000 copies
Reprint	July	2001	-	2000 copies
Reprint	October	2002	-	1000 copies
Reprint	February	2003	-	2000 copies
Reprint	October	2005	-	2000 copies

Published by:
CENTRAL CHINMAYA MISSION TRUST
Sandeepany Sadhanalaya
Saki Vihar Road,
Mumbai - 400 072, INDIA.
Tel: 91-22-28572367 / 28575806
Fax: 91-22-28573065
Email: ccmt@vsnl.com
Website: www.chinmayamission.com

Distribution Centre in USA:
CHINMAYA MISSION WEST
Publications Division,
560 Bridgetown Pike,
Langhorne, PA 19053, USA.
Tel: (215) 396-0390
Fax: (215) 396-9710
Email: publications@chinmaya.org
Website: www.chinmayapublications.org

Printed by
SAGAR UNLIMITED
28-B, Nand-Deep Industrial Estate,
Kondivita Lane, Andheri Kurla Road,
Mumbai-400 059.
Tel.: 28362777 / 28227699

Price: Rs. 25=00

ISBN 81-7597-334-X

Preface to the Revised Edition

Vedānta (*Veda* + *anta* i.e. the end of *Vedā-s*) as the literal meaning connotes comprises of the philosophical portion of the *Vedā-s* called the *Upaniṣad*-s. Of about 280 *Upaniṣad*-s unearthed so far, 108 have been accepted as athentic texts, and out of them eleven have been commented upon by the recent master-minds, *Ācāryā-s* like *Śrī Śaṅkara*, *Rāmānuja* and *Madhavācārya* and are thus classified as 'Major.'

The other *Upaniṣad-s* are considered as 'Minor'—not an account of their contents, or in the depth of their thoughts, or in the completeness of their exposition but because no commentaries are available from the great *Ācāryā*-s. The new initiates are generally prescribed these minor *Upaniṣad-s* only after a thorough study of the exhaustive commentaries *(Bhāṣyā-s)* by the great Masters on five or six of the Major *Upaniṣad-s*. Thus, these became 'minor' only with reference to the knowledge the students have already acquired as a result of their study of the "main" *Upaniṣad-s* and their reflection on these 'minor' ones serves as an interesting revision of the knowledge already gathered.

Kaivalya Upaniṣad belongs to the *Atharvaṇa Veda.* Its poetic diction, systematic development of thought—at once clear, concise and scientific arrangement of highly philosophical ideas make it one the most striking minor *Upaniṣad-s.*

Śatarudrīya is a prayer of hundred stanzas very sacred and inspiring involving *Rudra* i.e. Lord *Śiva,* which forms part of *Taittirīya Saṁhitā* of the *Yajur Veda* and was repeated by devotees with ardent faith and total dedication during the *Vedik* period. The great commentator *Nārāyaṇa* calls the *Kaivalya*

Upaniṣad as the *Brahma-Śatarudrīya* i.e. the *Śatarudrīya* which glorifies the unconditioned *Brahman* as opposed to the Personal God, Lord *Śiva*.

True to the *Upaniṣadik* style where Masters consider the story form as a conversation between the teacher and his disciple as the most apt devise to make the subject easily intelligible; in this *Upaniṣad Aśvalāyana,* the great teacher of *Ṛg Veda* is a disciple and Lord *Brahmā,* the Creator himself is the teacher, which makes this as the most valuable amongst the 'minor' *Upaniṣad-s*.

Repeated reprints had resulted in numerous inaccuracies rendering understanding difficult for new *Sādhakā-s*. Besides readability was poor in small print. Both these aspects are taken care of in the revised layout, the credit for which is due to Shri Vishwamitra Puri who with consistent perseverance and devotion scrutinised the entire book very minutely to identify misprints, missing words and lines; added diacritical marks and pursued steadfastly, the suggested changes/improvements, with the *Ācārya* of *Sāndīpany* Mumbai for approval.

In this revised Edition diacritical marks are used for Transliteration of *Saṁskṛta* words in the verses as well as commentary. In the 'word-for-word meaning' section also, for benefit of readers not knowing *Devanāgarī,* transliteration of *Saṁskṛta* words is added. Non-English words have been italicised. In the 'free translation' section where the entire text is italicised, to distinguish *Saṁskṛta* words, 'normal' fonts are used. This will help readers to identify and pronounce the words correctly.

The English plural sign 's' has been added to the untranslated *Saṁskṛta* words after a hyphen (-) to show that it is not elemental to the word e.g., *mantrā-s, Vedā-s, Ṛṣī-s* etc. Macrons are used on the last letter e.g. *'ā, ī'* of such words to lengthen the quantity of sound in consonance with the pronunciation.

To be true to the *Saṁskṛta* text in transliteration, we have used "*brāhmaṇa*" for the first *Varṇa* instead of the commonly used word "*brāhmin.*" It need not be confused with the term "*Brahman*" of the *Vedāntin*-s.

A key to the transliteration and pronunciation is added in the beginning and Alphabetical Index to *Mantrā*-s at the end of the book.

We are pleased to bring out the present revised Edition of the original commentary given by *H. H. Svāmī Chinmayananda* whom we all reverentially refer as *Pūjya Gurudeva*. This is our humble offering at His holy feet with a prayer that may His words and guidance inspire us to carry on His work in all spheres of activities such as this---publication of scriptural thoughts for the benefit of the society.

Vijayādaśamī : 11th October, 1997. Publishers

TRANSLITERATION AND PRONNUCIATION GUIDE

ॐ	oṁ	home	ॐ	oṁ	Rome
अ	a	fun	ट	ṭa	touch
आ	ā	car	ठ	ṭha	ant-hill
इ	i	pin	ड	ḍa	duck
ई	ī	feen	ढ	ḍha	godhood
उ	u	put	ण	ṇa	thunder
ऊ	ū	pool	त	ta	(close to) think
ऋ	ṛ	rig	थ	tha	(close to) pathetc
ॠ	ṝ	(long ṛ)	द	da	(close to) father
ऌ	ḷ	*	ध	dha	(close to) breathe hard
ए	e	play	न	na	numb
ऐ	ai	high	प	pa	purse
ओ	o	over	फ	pha	sapphire
औ	au	cow	ब	ba	but
अं	aṁ	**	भ	bha	abhor
अः	aḥ	***	म	ma	mother
क	ka	kind	य	ya	young
ख	kha	blockhead	र	ra	run
ग	ga	gate	ल	la	luck
घ	gha	log-hut	व	va	virtue
ङ	ṅa	sing	श	śa	shove
च	ca	chunk	ष	ṣa	bushel
छ	cha	match	स	sa	sir
ज	ja	jug	ह	ha	house
झ	jha	hedgehog	ळ	(Note 1)	(close to) wiorld
ञ	ña	bunch	क्ष	kṣa	worksheet
त्र	tra	three	ज्ञ	jña	*
ऽ		unpronounced (a)	ऽऽ	"	Unpronounced (ā)

Note 1: "ḷ" itself is sometimes used. * No English Equivalent.
** Nasaḷisation of the preceding vowel. *** Aspiration of preceding vowel

KAIVALYOPANIṢAD

(Minor *Upaniṣad*)

Introduction

The philosophical portion of the *Vedā-s* is called the *Upaniṣad-s*. They are found appended to all the four *Veda* volumes, and thus we have *Upaniṣad-s* belonging to the *Ṛg Veda*; some belonging to the *Yajur Veda*; others are found in the *Sāma Veda,* and yet others in the *Atharvaṇa Veda*.

Each *Vedik* text book reveals its contents under four sections:

(a) The *Mantra* portion, containing lyrical poems of exquisite charm describing and adoring the beauty of nature and the power of the phenomenal forces;

(b) The *Brāhmaṇa* section containing the ritualistic injunctions and prescriptions for the various ceremonies;

(c) The *Āraṇyakā-s*, containing various methods of meditation called the *Upāsanā-s*; and

(d) The *Upaniṣad-s*, containing the philosophical discussions that had taken place at various periods of time between different teachers and their students, regarding the Eternal Purpose of Creation and the Great Goal of Existence.

The very term '*Upa-ni-ṣad*' has a very purposeful meaning and deep significance, indicating the contents, nature and use of this literature. The Western scholars derive "*Upa-ni-ṣad*" from the word '*ṣad*' meaning to sit. When this word '*ṣad*' is preceded by the prepositions '*ni*' meaning 'down,' and '*upa*' meaning 'near,' then the '*Upa-ni-ṣad*' comes to mean the "near down-sit-literature." The term naturally describes the literature as that which cannot be directly learnt by the student from any given text books, but it is necessary that he should approach a teacher, sit "near" in front of him "down" in an attitude of reverence and devotion, and listen to the teacher's expositions.

However, the Indian scholars give a deeper significance to the term "*Upa-ni-ṣad.*" By reading the word '*ṣad*' to mean "destruction," the term '*Upa-ni-ṣad*' means a literature that destroys our present ignorance of Reality by revealing the experience of the Supreme; and when '*ṣad*' means 'approach,' then the term indicates that it is a literature that helps the student to *approach* or to *attain* the Supreme Wisdom.

Altogether there are about 280 *Upaniṣad-s* so far unearthed, and the scholars are still continuing their research in fixing up their authenticity and the relative dates of their composition, and, therefore, the chronology of their development. Hundred and eight of them have already been accepted by the *Paṇḍita*-class as orthodox and authentic texts. Of these 108 *Upaniṣad-s*, eleven have been commented upon by the recent master-minds, the *Ācaryā-s* like *Śrī Śaṅkara*, *Rāmānuja* and *Madhava*. Because of the exhaustive and learned exposition by these master-minds, the eleven *Upaniṣad-s* have become naturally, the most important texts for the students.

Relatively therefore, the *Upaniṣad-s* other than these eleven are considered as *minor* ones. It must be particularly noted that they are not *minor* ones in their contents or in the depth of their thoughts or in the completeness of their exposition. They are *minor* only with reference to the knowledge the students have already gathered from the eleven *Upaniṣad-s* with the help of the famous exhaustive *Bhāṣyā-s*.

In fact, some of the Minor *Upaniṣad-s*, with their revealing expressions and vivid terms of exposition throw a flood of light to illuminate some of the unrevealed corners in the major eleven *Upaniṣad-s*. Very often the Minor *Upaniṣad-s* repeat the stanzas and *mantrā-s* of the Major *Upaniṣad-s*. In short, after a complete study of the elaborate commentaries that open up the intricate philosophical categories of *Hindūism*, as expounded in the Major *Upaniṣad-s*, to all serious students, these texts become, in fact, *elementary* and *minor:* elementary in contents and minor in stature.

These *Upaniṣad-s* are generally prescribed for all students who have already gone through an extensive study of at least five or six of the "Major" *Upaniṣad-s*. For them reflection upon the "Minor" *Upaniṣad-s* becomes, as it were, an interesting revision of what they had already gathered from the "main" *Upaniṣad-s*.

The *Upaniṣad-s* are not creedal. They are not the hasty declaration of a man-of-wisdom under some divine urge. They, in themselves, constitute a science—the Science of Life. Just, as in Physics, we have many Scientists, each one adding to the total knowledge of the world-of-objects by his own theories and discoveries, we have in the *Upaniṣadik* lore an array of mighty men, who had enriched its contents by their dedicated investigations in, contemplation upon, and discoveries on the Sources of Life. The Scriptural Realm was thus opened up by them, and each *Upaniṣad* invites the student to enter into this glorious world of Light and Knowledge, of Peace and Perfection.

No blind promises are found anywhere in the *Upaniṣad-s*. Never do the *Ṛṣī-s* fanatically insist upon any belief. At every stage they closely observe and analyse the known, and very logically deduce the possibilities of the Unknown, and thereafter, they prescribe techniques by which the students can grow themselves into a state of unfoldment in themselves, wherein they too can come to experience what the *Upaniṣad* theories insist upon.

The *Kaivalya Upaniṣad* belongs to the *Atharvaṇa Veda* and it is one of the striking *Upaniṣad-s* among the "Minor" ones, especially because of its poetic diction, systematic development of thought, scientific arrangement of ideas, as also due to the comprehension of its vision and the richness of its philosophy. There is neither the jarring note of repetition, nor the cumbersome burden of redundancy. Spun from pure philosophy, carefully corded with subjective experience, the ideas weave themselves into a vivid pattern of the attractive Reality.

Here too, faithful to the *Upaniṣad*-tradition, we have a student approaching a teacher demanding Knowledge. It must be noted that the student here is not of the average type nor is the teacher anyone other than the very Creator (*Brahmā*) Himself.

Naturally, therefore, there is no beating about the bush here in the text. The teacher directly approaches the problem, and with minimum words the entire picture of evolution of man and the subtle techniques of attaining the State of Self-realisation have been revealed.

Śānti Pāṭha

ॐ भद्रं कर्णेभिः श‍ृणुयाम देवाः भद्रं पश्येमाक्षभिर्यजत्राः।
स्थिरैरङ्गैस्तुष्टुवाग्ं सस्तनूभिः व्यशेम देवहितं यदायुः॥
स्वस्ति न इन्द्रो वृद्धश्रवाः स्वस्ति नः पूषा विश्ववेदाः।
स्वस्ति नस्तार्क्ष्यो अरिष्टनेमिः स्वस्ति नो बृहस्पतिर्दधातु॥

ॐ शान्तिः शान्तिः शान्तिः ॥

Oṁ bhadraṁ karṇebhiḥ śṛṇuyāma devāḥ
bhadraṁ paśyem-ākṣabhir-yajatrāḥ,
sthirair-aṅgais-tuṣṭuvāgṁ-sastanūbhiḥ`
vyaśema devahitaṁ yadāyuḥ.
svasti na indro vṛddha-śravāḥ
svasti naḥ pūṣā viśva-vedāḥ,
svasti nastārkṣyo ariṣṭanemiḥ
svasti no bṛhaspatir-dadhātu.

Oṁ Śāntiḥ ! Śāntiḥ !! Śāntiḥ !!!

भद्रम् *bhadram* = What is auspicious; कर्णेभिः *karṇebhiḥ* = by ears; श‍ृणुयाम *śṛṇuyāma* = may we hear; देवाः *devāḥ* = Oh! Gods; भद्रम् *bhadram* = auspicious; पश्येम *paśyema* = may we see; अक्षभिः *akṣabhiḥ* = by eyes; यजत्राः *yajatrāḥ* = Oh worshipped ones; स्थिरैः *sthiraiḥ* = hale and hearty; अङ्गैः *aṅgaiḥ* = by the limbs; तुष्टवागम् सः *tuṣṭuvāgm saḥ* = may we live offering our praises (Unto Thee); तनूभिः *tanūbhiḥ* = by the body; व्यशेम *vyaśema* = may we have; देवहितम् *devahitam* = for the benefit of the *devā-s;* यत् आयुः *yat āyuḥ* = (lit. whatever) entire span of life; स्वस्ति *svasti* = blessings; नः *naḥ* = to us; इन्द्रः *indraḥ* = *Indra*; वृद्ध-श्रवाः *vṛddha śravāḥ* = ancient and famous; स्वस्ति *svasti* = blessings; नः *naḥ* = to us; पूषा *pūṣā* = Sun;

विश्ववेदा: *viśva-vedāḥ* = the all-knowing; स्वस्ति *svasti* = blessings; न: *naḥ* = to us; तार्क्ष्य: *tārkṣyaḥ* = Lord of Swift Motion (*Vāyu*); अरिष्टनेमि: *ariṣṭanemiḥ* = who saves (us) from harm; स्वस्ति *svasti* = blessings; न: *naḥ* = to us; बृहस्पति: *bṛhaspatiḥ* = *Bṛhaspati* (Protector of the spiritual wealth in us, the Lord of Prayers); दधातु *dadhātu* = may (He) give.

ओम् *Oṁ* = symbol of *Parā Brahman*; शान्ति: *śāntiḥ* = peace be; शान्ति: *śāntiḥ* = peace be; शान्ति: *śāntiḥ* = peace be.

1. *O ye Gods, may we hear with our ears (always) what is auspicious; O Worshipful Ones, may we with our eyes see (always) what is auspicious. May we live the entire length of our allotted life hale and hearty, offering our praises (unto Thee). May* Indra, *the ancient and the famous, Sun* (Pūṣān) *the all-knowing, the Lord of Swift Motion (*Vāyu*) who saves us from all harms, and* Bṛhaspati *who protects the spiritual wealth in us—bless us (with the intellectual strength to understand the scriptures and the heroic heart to follow the teachings.)*

Oṁ Peace be! Peace be!! Peace be!!!

No *Upaniṣad*-study ever started without the *guru* and the disciple chanting together the peace-invocation. Everyday the teacher and the taught sat together and started their discourses only after a common prayer.

Each one of us is not merely an intellectual, fearful, ever sighing, limited creature; but has within ourselves a personality supremely omnipotent, fearless, unlimited, all blissful and Godly. Prayer is the technique by which we tune ourselves to the highest perfection and thereby come to invoke in ourselves a greater perfection of both the mind and the intellect.

"To pray is to be seated with the Lord at His feet. To pray is to aim at the target of God-head with the arrow of intense longing, which has the sharp end of full faith. To pray is, again, to receive consolation and inspiration as a disciple at the hands of the teacher." In prayer are included praise, love, adoration and glorification.

Just before the study of the *Upaniṣad*-s, thus each day, the Master and the disciple pray, and thus invoke the best in them to come out, through a complete surrender to the mighty powers of an Omniscient God-principle.

Every word in the *Śānti Pāṭha* is a declaration hinting at the vicious criminal instincts in ourselves. We have started employing Gods, through prayers, as our advocates, commission agents, doctors and even abetters in our murderous intentions. This is not a fault of the technique. A dagger can be used in murdering the mother or protecting the family. If one vicious man murders his mother in a moment of antagonism, because of that we cannot declare that the dagger is a cruel weapon. Similarly, the technique of prayer is a blessing; but it is we, who, by employing it for low purposes, vitiate the very institution of prayer.

The great Masters in the *Upaniṣad*-s knew no desire for the sense-world which they had enquired into and discovered to be hollow and riddled with carping sorrows. They prayed only for the cultural evolution of the entire kingdom of beings. This national character of the *Vedik* period is stamped so faithfully in the words of the *Śānti* stanza in each of the *Upaniṣad*-s. Both the Master and disciple sincerely wished and prayed that they should, during their spiritual life, see and hear nothing but auspiciousness. The sense-organs—the eyes and ears are the great grand-trunk-roads through which Satan enters the realm of the Godly, within man. The other sense objects do not so directly pave a way to the mental suicides in man. Both the outer scenes of viciousness and the inner murmurs of foul intentions directly sweep us in front of them and then defile the edifice of spiritualism in our bosom; hence the great prayer of the *Vedik* seers that they should hear and see nothing but goodness and purity.

Here in the prayer of the *Vedik* Masters, we have the Das Capita of the *Hindū*-s. If each one, in a society or a community, is to ardently and sincerely pray so as to meet with only auspiciousness and act for the same, in such a country at such an era of culture, jails will be redundant, slum areas will be unknown, poverty unimaginable, disease a mere exception. From the state of affairs available today, we may despair and fail even to visualise that such a perfect spiritual communism would ever be possible in the world, but this seems to be the pattern aimed at by the *Ṛṣī*-s of old and their prayers clearly indicate to what perfections they brought their visions, in their own times, as facts realised.

Again, not only they lived in a spirit of complete renunciation and acted on the principle of universal love, but that perfect generation, perfect in every sense of the term, was never blind to the necessities of the physical and the material world. They never complained of life. With an appetite, they wooed life and were ever impatient in their thirst for more of it; this is evident from their prayers, that the Lord of the Universe must bless them to live *the entire span of life allotted* to them in all health and perfect vitality.

Their invocations to *Indra*, *Vāyu* (Air), *Sūrya* (Sun) etc., make us remember that *Rāma* and *Kṛṣṇa*—Gods are the products of a much later age. They were deities that were sanctioned in the *Paurāṇik* times. In the *Vedik* period, the Masters knew only the five Great Elements and such other manifestations to be the Divine personalities, the *Devatā*-s. They are invoked here both by the *Guru* and the disciple.

No peace-invocation concludes without thrice repeating or invoking *Śānti*. The three repetitions are, it is explained by the *Ācāryā*-s, addressed to the three groups in which all the probable obstacles in the study of the scriptures can be classified. They are the God-sent *(Ādhi-daivika)*, such as Lightning, thunder; or phenomenal *(Ādhi-bhautika)* such as fires, floods and land slides etc; or purely subjective *(Ādhyātmika)* such as inertia, lack of faith, insincerity and such others that arise from our own negativities.

KAIVALYOPANIṢAD

Chapter 1

ॐ अथाश्वलायनो भगवन्तं परमेष्ठिनमुपसमेत्योवाच–

Oṁ Athāśvalāyano bhagavantaṁ parameṣṭhinam-upasamety-ovāca-

Then *Āśvalāyana* approached Lord *Parameṣṭhi*, (the Creator, *Brahmā*) and said :

Āśvalāyana is a famous teacher in the *Ṛg Veda* and many are his *Mantrā-s* that go into the bulk of our accepted *Hindū* Sacred Books. He is such a great teacher who is approaching the greatest Master, to gain a fuller confirmation for himself and if possible, more light upon the Truth. The teacher here in this *Upaniṣad*, is the Creator, *Brahmā* who was Himself the first teacher who taught the spiritual Wisdom to his first-born sons, the *Sanat Kumārā-s*. Therefore, we understand that here we have a great student approaching the greatest of teachers, seeking Wisdom. Naturally, therefore, the standard of discussion in the *Upaniṣad* cannot be cheap, or the thoughts rambling.

The term "then" (*Atha*) is a typical phrase used in the scriptural literature of India. The *Brahma-sūtrā-s*[1] start with the same word "*Atha.*" In all these places, the word then indicates a time when the student has already undergone all the previous disciplines, that are unavoidable in order to make him fit for the study of this delicate science. Self-analysis, contemplation upon the transcendental and the experience of

1. "*Athato Brahma Jijñāsā*" is the opening *sūtra* of the *Brahma sūtrā-s* of *Śrī Vyāsa Bhagavān*.

the Absolute are not readily open for everyone. A certain amount of preparation is unavoidable.

The opening word of the *Upaniṣad* "then" indicates that the student *Āśvalāyana* has already prepared himself with all the necessary qualification* such as the spirit of discrimination (*Viveka*), power of detachment (*Vairāgya*), the six rules of self-control and self-discipline (*Ṣaṭ-Sampatti*) and a burning aspiration to liberate himself from the thraldom of matter (*Mumukṣutvam*) and therefore, he is ready to receive the great knowledge.

अधीहि भगवन् ब्रह्मविद्यां वरिष्ठां
सदा सद्भिः सेव्यमानां निगूढाम् ।
ययाऽचिरात् सर्वपापं व्यपोह्य
परात्परं पुरुषं याति विद्वान् ॥ १ ॥

Adhīhi bhagavan brahma-vidyāṁ variṣṭhāṁ
sadā sadbhiḥ sevyamānāṁ nigūḍhām,
yayā'cirāt sarva-pāpaṁ vyapohya
parāt-paraṁ puruṣaṁ yāti vidvān.

अधीहि *adhīhi* = teach; भगवन् *bhagavan* = O! Lord, ब्रह्म-विद्याम् *brahma-vidyām* = *Brahma-vidyā*, metaphysics; वरिष्ठाम् *variṣṭhām* = highest; सदा *sadā* = always; सद्भिः *sadbhiḥ* = by the good people; सेव्यमानाम् *sevyamānam* = being resorted to; निगूढाम् *nigūḍham* = secret; यया *yayā* = by which; अचिरात् *acirāt* = soon; सर्व-पापम् *sarva-pāpam* = all sins; व्यपोह्य *vyapohya* = discarding; परात्-परम् *parāt-param* = the highest; पुरुषम् *puruṣam* = *Puruṣa*—the Self; याति *yāti* = goes; विद्वान् *vidvān* = wise.

1. *O!* Bhagavan, *teach me the highest Science of Reality, cultivated always by the good people, which is ever a hidden secret for man, a knowledge by which a wise man, discarding all sins, can reach the Highest* "Puruṣa."

* Refer Talks on *Vivekacūḍāmaṇī* verses 20-27 by *Svāmījī*.

When a fully qualified student reaches the feet of a teacher, it is always the duty of the student to express his doubts. Then alone will the teacher open his mouth to discuss and try to clear the doubt. In many of the *Upaniṣad-s* we read the seeker's question, and even where it is not explicitly expressed, from the very trend of the teacher's answer, it becomes obvious that the student had definitely expressed a doubt of his own.

Āśvalāyana's request was that Lord *Brahmā* should teach him the Science of Reality, called *Brahma-vidyā*. It is the Science of all sciences in as much as this Knowledge makes all other scientists and professional better men in their own fields-of-knowledge. The Science of *Brahman* reveals the Supreme Consciousness, which illumines the ideas and thoughts in all intellects. To unveil this Consciousness and thus bring a clearer flood of light into the bosom would be automatically sharpening the quality of all other thinkers and scientists.

Āśvalāyana himself indicates why he has sought a teacher for instructions in this Science. All other sciences can, perhaps, to a great extent, be studied directly from some available text books that explain the knowledge of it, if one has the necessary industry and self-application. But in the spiritual field books cannot give us the knowledge; for language cannot explain that which words cannot define. Nor can this Reality be perceived by any man, however intelligent he may be, all by himself. It is a great hidden knowledge (*Nigūḍhām*).

By the term "secret," it is not meant that it is a knowledge that "cannot be given out to others"; it only means that it is a knowledge which will be beyond our comprehension until we are initiated into it by some experienced teacher.

The *Hindū* Philosophy is not satisfied by merely giving a theological exposition of what can be the final Reality, but it tries its best to charter for us a way-of-life by which we can come to apprehend subjectively the Ultimate Truth. At the moment of this awakening into the plane of God-consciousness, the individual can no longer be functioning through his equipments of matter—the body, the mind and the intellect.

These matter-vehicles have been projected in order to express the existing *Vāsanā-s* and to create new ones in us. When an individual succeeds in transcending his "perceiver-feeler-thinker-personality," he must necessarily go beyond all his self-accumulated *Vāsanā-s.*

The *Vāsanā-s* are called Sin (*Pāpa*). Sin is that which causes mental fluttering and intellectual agitations. All *Vāsanā-s*, as long as they exist, will by their reactions, ever try to express themselves in the form of thoughts, feelings and actions. Naturally, therefore, the Science of *Brahman* is such that through its practice when we ultimately come to experience the Self in us, we would have, by then, gone beyond all the "sins" (*Pāpā-s* or *Vāsanā-s*).

Not only do we, at the moment of Self-realisation transcend the vehicles of our expression and experience, not only do we then go beyond the very cause of these agitations namely the *Vāsanā-s,* but we shall also have thereby a positive experience of the Transcendental *Puruṣa.*

The student is here demanding that knowledge by which he can transcend his Causal-body* and come to apprehend and live the Universal Truth, the one Life Eternal which expresses itself as a universe of multiple forms and names.

तस्मै स होवाच पितामहश्च–
'श्रद्धाभक्तिध्यानयोगादवैहि' ॥ २ ॥

Tasmai sa hovāca pitāmahaś-ca-
'śraddhā-bhakti-dhyāna-yogād-avaihi'

तस्मै *tasmai* = to him; स *sa* = He; ह *ha* = verily; उवाच *uvāca* = said; पितामहः *pitāmahaḥ* = Grandsire; च *ca* = and; श्रद्धा भक्ति ध्यान योगात्

* Refer *Māṇḍūkya and Kārikā,* and *Ātma Bodha*. The entire bundle of *Vāsanā-s* in us, the Vehicle in which we express ourselves in deep sleep, constitutes our Causal Body.

śraddhā-bhakti-dhyāna-yogāt = by means of faith, devotion and meditation; अवैहि *avaihi* = know.

2. *To him the Grandsire* (Brahmā) *said, "Know this by means of faith, devotion and meditation."*

When a teacher is properly approached by a deserving student, and when the student has placed at the feet of his teacher his great doubt on the transcendental theme, the teacher is by duty bound to explain,* as best as he can, the Science of Life, and thus relieve the student of his mental confusions. The part that the teacher has to play is unenviable indeed. He has to address the student's intellect—awaken in him his powers of creative thinking, guide his thoughts to the very uttermost limits of thinking and later on, help him to reach the kingdom of the Pure Self. This Process of Self-unfoldment, along the guided path, is to be walked indeed by the student himself, if he is to succeed in the subjective quest of Truth.

All these implications and technical difficulties in teaching Spiritual Knowledge were known to the student *Āśvalāyana*, because he himself was already a teacher. Therefore, in the shortest number of words the teacher, *Brahmā* here, indicates the instrument of evolution and the technique of Self-unfoldment in the very opening words of his answer.

Thus *Brahma-vidyā*, the Science of Life, is to be understood, according to the stanza, "by means of faith (*Śraddhā*), and meditation (*Dhyāna*). The statement is very significant. Faith has been described as "that faculty of the human intellect by which it can reflect and understand the deeper imports of the scriptural declarations and thereafter assimilate those ideas into the very texture of the intellect." This power of understanding and assimilating new ideas, so as to evolve itself, is called *Śraddhā*. Thus essentially, *Śraddhā* is the function of the intellect. It is the power for Self-education.

---

* In *Vivekacūḍāmaṇī* (Section 10 - verse 41 to 47) *Śaṅkara* makes it clear that a teacher must immediately quieten the student's agitation and teach him the knowledge of the Greater Life.

Devotion is love directed towards a higher ideal whereby the devotee gains an unfoldment, experiences an upliftment and thus come to outshine his own capabilities. This is essentially a function of the heart; the Temple of Love is ever in the heart.

If faith (*Śraddhā*) is the function of the intellect, and devotion (*Bhakti*) is the function of the heart, then meditation (*Dhyāna*) is an integrated act of both the head and the heart. When the intellectual aspect in our personality, nurtured and nourished by the higher ideals (Faith), and the heart elevated and inspired by its dedication to these very same principles (Devotion) function together, it becomes the act of meditation (*Dhyāna*). The prepared head intellectually moving forward conquering new possibilities and the heart endowed with devotion, following at its heels to consolidate the conquest through its identification—this combined action of both the head and the heart is called meditation.

The declarations of the *Upaniṣad-s* are at best a vain attempt to define the indefinable, to explain the inexplicable, to understand the un-understandable. Since the theme of the *Upaniṣad-s* is the subjective Self, which is a realm of experience that lies beyond the frontiers of the intellect, all learned theoretical discussions, or shared intellectual comprehensions, must necessarily fall short of the subjective experience. But at the same time the teacher can instruct and the taught can study only from the level of the intellect. Therefore, the great teacher *Brahmā* here in the *Upaniṣad*, at its very opening, warns the student that this Great Knowledge can be gained not by the usual channel of understanding, but by a special secret technique.

That which cannot be experienced by the heart, can often be comprehended by the intellect in our ordinary life. Scientific theories or economic programmes are examples of knowledge that can be intellectually comprehended even though it cannot be emotionally experienced. But, if there be a Truth which can either be physically seen or emotionally felt or intellectually thought of, it is to be apprehended by an integration of all our existing faculties. This power of apprehension, arising out of a combination of all our faculties is called *intuition*. The harmonised head and heart develop in themselves a power of perception which is not the sum total of their faculties; it transcends them and *this power of subjective perception in man is called intuition.*

In short, the teacher warns the student that unlike other sciences of the world, spiritual knowledge cannot come through the head or the heart, but it can be experienced only through the faculty of intuition, which is to be cultivated by the student for himself.

न कर्मणा न प्रजया धनेन त्यागेनैके अमृतत्वमानशुः ।
परेण नाकं निहितं गुहायां विभ्राजते यद्यतयो विशन्ति ॥३॥

Na karmaṇā na prajayā dhanena
tyāgenaike amṛtatvam-ānaśuḥ,
pareṇa nākaṁ nihitaṁ guhāyāṁ
vibhrājate yad-yatayo viśanti.

न *na* = not; कर्मणा *karmaṇā* = by work; न *na* = not; प्रजया *prajayā* = by progeny; धनेन *dhanena* = by wealth; त्यागेन *tyāgena* = by renunciation; एके *eke* = alone; अमृतत्वम् *amṛtatvam* = immortality; आनशुः *ānaśuḥ* = attained; परेण *pareṇa* = higher than; नाकम् *nākam* = heaven; निहितम् *nihitam* = kept; गुहायाम् *guhāyām* = in the cave (of the intellect); विभ्राजते *vibhrājate* = shines; यत् *yat* = which; यतयः *yatayaḥ* = self-controlled sages; विशन्ति *viśanti* = enter.

3. *Not by work, nor by progeny, nor by wealth, but by renunciation alone, Immortality is attained. Higher than heaven, seated in the cave of the intellect, It shines, which the seekers attain.*

That the theme of the *Upaniṣad* can be experienced only through intuition has been already explained. To confirm that idea, here the teacher totally denies all effectiveness for other methods-of-acquisitions, in gaining the Supreme Self of the *Upaniṣad-s*. By action and work* we generally strive for and acquire the world-of-objects; sometimes an amount of happiness can be gained through the success of or even by the indirect help of those who depend upon us (*Prajayā*); an amount of happiness can be really ordered by wealth.

Direct effort, indirect help, purchase by wealth—these are the three avenues through which we come to our worldly success and happiness. We achieve happiness in daily life either through our *self-effort* (*Karmaṇā*), or sometimes our self-efforts are supplemented by the help we get from others (*Prajayā*) and at other times, we gain happiness by purchasing it with wealth (*Dhanena*). None of these methods of transaction, which are available in the world-of-objects, can bring to us the spiritual solace or the subjective Wisdom.

The world-of-objects is apprehended and experienced only through the instruments of the body, mind and intellect. Through the body we *percieve* the world of objects, through the mind we *feel* the emotions, through the intellect we *think* of our ideas and ideals. The theme that has been explained and expounded in the *Upaniṣad-s*, ***Brahman*** is not something that falls under the world-of-objects constituted of the perceptions, the feelings or the thoughts, but it is that Effulgent Consciousness that illumines them all. This Supreme, Divine Subject in us, that presides over us, as our own Self, can be apprehended only in the subjective experience, at a time when we are not functioning through our body or mind or intellect.

Therefore, the above statement indicates that by liquidating our identification with the body, mind and intellect alone can we reach "the still moment of meditation" and therein alone can we awaken ourselves to the Universal Truth. To detach ourselves from the false perceptions, and their apparent joys and sorrows is true renunciation (*Tyāga*).

---

* Work done with the motive of gaining sense-gratifications, i.e. *Sakāma Karma* is meant here and not *Niṣkāma Karma* i.e. Selfless work which helps to remove bondage...Ed.

A child looking out into the world through a blue glass will certainly see the world blue. In order to see the world as it is, if the child changes his blue glass-piece to a red, green or yellow one, it will not serve the purpose. For when viewed through the different coloured glass-pieces his vision will be coloured by the very colour of glass-pieces and to look at the world with the naked eye is the only method to apprehend the world as it is.

Similarly, in order to recognise the Truth if we look at through the body, we can only experience the world constituted by so many different stimuli; through the mind, it is interpreted as so many emotions; through the intellect it can be experienced only as thoughts and ideas. In order to recognise the Reality behind the world these distorting instruments of perception should be transcended—*renunciation alone is the true method.**

At such moments when the individual is no more functioning through his equipments-of-matter, at a time when one is neither perceiving, nor feeling, nor thinking, his individuality melts itself in the experience of the Universal Eternal Reality in him.

This great experience is termed in our *Upaniṣad-s* as the "State of Immortality." It is no doubt, a confusing term until the student is initiated into its special connotation. Change is mortality or death. Change not only indicates a new condition, but implies at once the end or destruction of its previous condition of existence. Thus, when morning changes to noon, it is not only the birth of the noon, but it is also at once the death of the morning. In every change the previous condition must die. A chain of such death-and-birth constitutes the "realms of change."

Finitude is experienced when we recognise the world-of-objects through the instruments of the body, mind and intellect. Transcending these three, we awaken ourselves to the Self, the Eternal, wherein there is no more change, and therefore, that

* *"Tena Tyaktena Bhunjīthāḥ "*— refer discourses on *Īśāvāsya Upaniṣad mantra*-1.

experience is called the State of Immortality. The Experience of God-Consciousness is termed thus in our *Śāstrā-s* as the Experience of Immortality.

The Plane of Consciousness thus experienced within our bosom is indicated here by the closing two lines of the above *mantra*.

"Higher than heaven" :—Strictly following the style and diction of the *Upaniṣad*, here in these two lines, we get a beautiful description of the State of Immortality. In *Saṁskṛta*, '*Kam*' means 'Joy' and '*A-kam*' means 'Pain' and '*Na a-kam*' means 'No Pain'. This term 'No Pain' (*Nākam*) is employed in the *Upaniṣad* to indicate Heaven, meaning thereby that it is a "state beyond pain," but it is not a positive state of definite joy. This type of a negative condition is experienced by us in our deep-sleep condition when we are in our causal body, and we have therein the state of "No-Pain." The positive realm of spiritual glory defined here by the term "Immortality" is described as something higher than the negative state of "No-Pain" (*Pareṇa Nākam*).

"When am I to experience It? Where can the seeker search for it, so that he may come to apprehend It?" The stanza answers: "seated in the cave of the Intellect." It is a typical *Upaniṣadik* phrase, very often used extensively in this literature, and it has a special scientific significance. According to the *Upaniṣadik* lore, in the "cave of the heart" is the seat of the intellect, and the *Ṛṣī-s* continue to explain that in the "cave of the intellect" is the seat of the Self. When we are inside a cave, we all know that all around and about us it is nothing but the cave. In philosophy "heart" means the humane qualities of love, tenderness, mercy etc. A seeker must first of all develop those human qualities of the heart, and then his intellect can apprehend the very Consciousness which illumines all thoughts as the very Self. Remember, every science has got its own vocabulary and the *Ṛṣī-s* of old brought into their Subjective Science of Life the lyricism of their poetic minds.

"That which shines" (*Vibhrājate*):—In the "Cave of the heart" transcending even the state of sleep (No-Pain), is the plane of the God-Consciousness into which seekers readily enter (*Viśanti*).

वेदान्तविज्ञानसुनिश्चितार्थाः
संन्यासयोगाद्यतयः शुद्धसत्त्वाः ।
ते ब्रह्मलोकेषु परान्तकाले
परामृतात्परिमुच्यन्ति सर्वे ॥ ४ ॥

Vedānta-vijñāna-suniścitārthāḥ
saṁnyāsa-yogād-yatayaḥ śuddha-sattvāḥ,
te brahma-lokeṣu parānta-kāle
parāmṛtāt-parimucyanti sarve.

वेदान्त विज्ञान सुनिश्चितार्थाः *vedānta-vijñāna-suniścit-ārthāḥ* = those who have come to ascertain clearly the deeper imports of the knowledge of the *Vedānta* (*Upaniṣad-s*); संन्यास-योगात् *saṁnyāsa-yogāt* = through renunciation; यतयः *yatayaḥ* = self-controlled sages; शुद्ध सत्त्वाः *śuddha sattvāḥ* = pure in mind; ते *te* = they; ब्रह्म लोकेषु *brahma lokeṣu* = in the regions of *Brahmā*; परान्त काले *parānta kāle* = at the time of the final end; परामृतात् *parāmṛtāt* = due to Highest Immortality; परिमुच्यन्ति *parimucyanti* = get freed; सर्वे *sarve* = all.

4. *Those who are pure in mind, striving through the path of renunciation, come to ascertain clearly the deeper imports of the Knowledge, which is the theme of the* Upaniṣad-s (Vedānta); *they, in the end, gain the world of* Brahmā, *and liberating themselves from everything gain the Highest Immortality.*

This *Mantra* is a significant one from the *Muṇḍaka Upaniṣad* (III-ii-6). Those who are seekers, when they have relatively quietened the agitations of their minds, become more and more receptive to the subtler Truth that is indicated in the declarations of the scriptures. A mind that is fully agitated is considered, in the terminology of philosophy as "Impure" (*A-śuddha*). The steady mind, agitationless and alert, is called a "pure" (*Śuddha*) mind. In order to penetrate into the deeper depths of the spiritual significances in the scriptural texts, it is unavoidable that one should have a certain amount of mental serenity. Undivided devotion (*Upāsanā*) is the technique by which this "inner purity" (*Antaḥkaraṇa śuddhi*) is cultivated.

In order to make the mind steady, the wanderings of the mind are to be controlled. The mind wanders only towards things and situations to which it has developed clinging attachments. To detach our mind from such objects is called *Sannyāsa*. Again, we in our identification with our body-mind-intellect, project ourselves into the world of objects-emotions-thoughts, and thus open our minds to a psychological climate of withering storms and disturbances. To detach ourselves from our identifications with the matter-vehicles in us is the secret of increasing our purposeful mental serenity.

To renounce our attachments to the sense-objects, and thus come to control the reception of stimuli from the world outside, is true renunciation (*Sannyāsa*). This attitude of renunciation becomes impossible to the many because mind cannot remain without attaching itself to something or the other. In order to release the mind from the agitation-breeding preoccupations with the world-of-objects, it must be given another "point of attention" (*Lakṣya*). Attuning the mind with the concept of the Highest Reality, and thus heaving the mind from the world of dissipation is called *Yoga* (from the root *Yuj* = to join). Thus, this beautiful phrase, "Detachment through attachment" (*Sannyāsa Yoga*) has been coined in the *Upaniṣadik* Literature.

Through this practice—of attaching our attention to the Higher, and thereby gaining detachment from the lower—when the seekers develop their "inner purity" the mind grows richer in its receptivity, alertness, comprehension, and in its power of apprehension. Such trained minds become fit for plunging into the study of scriptures. The *Upaniṣad-s* are appended to the various *Vedā-s* at their close (*Anta*), and therefore that literature is called *Vedānta*. The *Vedānta* literature not only explains to us theoretically the Knowledge (*Jñāna*) of the Reality, but it explains to us various techniques by which it can become a subjective Knowledge of vivid Experience (*Vijñāna*). Thus, the study of the scriptures in itself is never complete until the theoretical Knowledge discussed therein becomes our subjective Experience. Then alone the true meaning (*Artha*) of the scriptural declarations becomes fully apprehended and determined (*Suniścitam*).

Such seekers, it is declared in the second half of the *Mantra*, experience in themselves a greater unfoldment. According to the degree of this experience gained, the *Upaniṣad-s* declare two types of realisation :

(a) Direct Experience of the Infinite, even while we are here, even while continuing in our physical embodiment—called *Jīvanmukti,* and

(b) The "Realisation by stages" (*Krama Mukti*), wherein the seeker after leaving his physical existence enters the realm of the Total Mind, the Creator—the world of the *Hiraṇyagarbha* called *Brahma Loka*—and there, while enjoying a subtle life of joys, prepares himself for the highest experience which he gains at the end of the dissolution (*Pralaya*).

Both these paths are laid out, chartered and described in the *Upaniṣadik* literature. Here, in the *mantra* under discussion, it is so worded that both these paths are indicated.

Those of the seekers, who have cultivated this inner purity and have come to experience fully the theme of the *Upaniṣad-s*, directly live in God-Consciousness, even while continuing apparently in their old physical structure. The term

Brahmaloka in *Saṁskṛta* can be dissolved in two ways. The plane of experience (*Loka*) which is itself *Brahman* or it can also be dissolved as the plane of experience in which the Creator, the Total Intellect, *Brahmā*, revels.

Para-anta-kāle —"At the final end" is the word meaning of this term. This can be interpreted as at the end of the world's dissolution (*Pralaya*) or subjectively at the end of the ego-centric existence; realisation in stages and immediate Eternal Experience are implied by this term.

Para-amṛtaḥ—This term also can be applied for both types of realisation. Liberated in Life (*Jīvan-muktā-s*) come to live that which lies beyond (*Para*) the very Essence of Immortality (*Amṛta*). Mortality and Immortality are two intellectual concepts and both of them are illumined by the Consciousness in us. The illuminator is always, we know, something other than the illumined. In this sense of the term, the Absolute is indicated as a Blazing Factor that transcends the very concepts of mortality and immortality. Such mighty Masters who have become one with the Self are naturally indicated here as those who have "gone beyond even Immortality" (*Para-amṛtaḥ*). They who had already reached the Plane of Consciousness called *Brahmaloka*, get themselves totally absorbed into the Supreme Reality at the Great *Pralaya*-time.

After this final experience of God-'Vision' the seeker forever becomes liberated from all bondages experienced by him till then because of his identification with matter, and he gets liberated totally from everything (*Pari-mucyanti sarve*).

When such convincing assertions are made by the teacher, the true student, who is ever a man of practical visions, comes to demand personal experience of the Truth. *Vedānta* laughs at any theory, however logical it may be, unless there be in it a scientific process visualised by which a diligent seeker can come to experience the Truth in himself. In all the *Upaniṣad-s*, we find not only the description of a "Vision of life," but also we get an exhaustive discussion of the technique of Self-realisation as a "way of life." True to this healthy tradition, here in the *Kaivalya Upaniṣad* also, we find exhaustive details regarding the way of life and technique by which the students can confirm the vision of the theory with their own inner experience. The path of meditation has been completely chalked out by a few strokes in the following stanzas.

विविक्तदेशे च सुखासनस्थः
शुचिः समग्रीवशिरःशरीरः   ।
अत्याश्रमस्थः सकलेन्द्रियाणि
निरुध्य भक्त्या स्वगुरुं प्रणम्य   ॥
हृत्पुण्डरीकं विरजं विशुद्धं
विचिन्त्य मध्ये विशदं विशोकम् ॥ ५ ॥

Vivikta-deśe ca sukhāsana-sthaḥ

śuciḥ sama-grīva-śiraḥ-śarīraḥ

atyāśrama-sthaḥ sakalendriyāṇi

nirudhya bhaktyā svaguruṁ praṇamya

hṛt-puṇḍarīkaṁ virajaṁ viśuddhaṁ

vicintya madhye viśadaṁ viśokam.

विविक्त-देशे *vivikta-deśe* = in a secluded place; च *ca* = and; सुखासन-स्थः *sukhāsana-sthaḥ* = resting in a comfortable posture; शुचिः *śuciḥ* = pure; सम-ग्रीव-शिर:-शरीरः *sama-grīva-śiraḥ-śarīraḥ* = with neck, head and body in one line held erect; अति-आश्रम-स्थः *ati-āśrama-sthaḥ* = in a mental attitude of *Sannyāsa*; सकल-इन्द्रियाणि *sakala-indriyāṇi* = all the senses; निरुध्य *nirudhya* = having controlled; भक्त्या *bhaktyā* = with devotion; स्व-गुरुम् *sva-gurum* = to one's own teacher; प्रणम्य *praṇamya* = saluting; हृत्पुण्डरीकम् *hṛt-puṇḍarīkam* = the lotus of the heart; विरजम् *virajam* = untainted; विशुद्धम् *viśuddham* = pure; विचिन्त्य *vicintya* = meditating; मध्ये *madhye* = inside; विशदम् *viśadam* = clear; विशोकम् *viśokam* = griefless.

5. *In an undisturbed place, clean and pure, resting in a comfortable posture, with neck, head and body held erect in one line, in a mental attitude of* Sannyāsa *having controlled all the senses, saluting ones own teacher mentally with reverence, meditate within the lotus of the heart (on* Brahman*), the Untainted, the Pure, the Clear and the Griefless.*

In an undisturbed place (*Vivikta deśe*):—the Subjective Science of Self-investigation that seeks to know the very Source of Life in us, can be pursued only through self-analysis and contemplation. The subtlety of the field-of-observation, the natural distractions of the mind, the habitual agitations in, and the consequent disturbance of the single pointed-ness in the intellect... are some of the hazards on the path of the contemplators. Naturally therefore, such contemplators or meditators must necessarily bring about a serene silence and quietude in their mind in order to ensure success in their efforts. The mind is distracted and disturbed by the compelling attraction of the outer world-of-objects and the irresistible inner desires that erupt from the intellect. In order to bring about the necessary quietude in the mind, therefore, the student is advised to select an undisturbed place for his practice.

Resting in an easy posture (*sukha-āsana-sthaḥ*):—In such a selected, relatively quiet place, where the crowds of stimuli, emanating from the outer world, reach us the least to disturb our mind, the Seeker of Truth (the *Sādhaka*) must sit down to meditate. While sitting down, it is necessary that we take to a simple comfortable posture, wherein the limbs will not get immediately benumbed, nor is there any physical strain, for, the limbs strained will be again a continuous disturbances for the mind.

In the *Upaniṣad-s* it is often repeated, and even insisted upon, that meditation is possible only in a sitting posture. To sit down is to relax the body. When the body is relaxed, the "rays" of the mind attending to the demands of the flesh are gathered together, and, when the mind has thus rolled upon itself, the world of objects, that it would have otherwise perceived by its functioning through the sense organs, also gets temporarily knocked out from the seeker's attention.

A relaxed body brings to function a more poignant and vigilant mind for the purpose of contemplation. It is very well known that in our ordinary language, we associate intelligent discussion with a relaxed body, especially in such familiar terms as "Let us sit down and discuss the matter." Conversely, it is also familiar with us that we become always stiffened in the body before we act : "Stand up and fight." Continuous mental and intellectual pursuit is possible only when the body is at rest.

"Clean and pure" (*Śuciḥ*):—Cleaniness for the spiritual seeker (*śuciḥ*) is both within and without. The place selected for meditation must be a clean and healthy spot where there is no possibility of any disturbances from ants, bugs, mosquitoes, flies etc. Not only the prayer-room must be clean, but the individual who is to meditate must be, at least for the time being, undressed of all desires and disappointments, hatred and jealousy which generally bring about a lot of inner restlessness, which are the impurities in the bosom. A clean mind, therefore, is a mind that has withdrawn itself from the fields-of-agitation and has come to surrender fully in devotion and love at the Feet of the Great Altar.

"With neck, head and body held erect in one line" (*Sama-grīva-śiraḥ-śarīraḥ*):—When a technique is described, it is necessary that it must include all the unavoidable fine adjustments and arrangements, so that the student may not miss the secret of the method. It is interesting to note how the great *Ṛṣī-s* were very thorough in their technology; and they considered this knowledge of the technique as a very important help for meditation. Here the teacher *Brahmā* is insisting that during the meditation the vertebral column must be held erect and perpendicular to the seat. By keeping the head, neck and trunk in one straight line, with the hip portion slightly brought forward, when the seeker is sitting down in a comfortable posture (*Āsana*)—with maximum base—the individual is in a "neutral" equilibrium-position wherein his centre-of-gravity would necessarily fall at his own base.*

After thus describing the necessary, helpful, arrangements of things around the meditator, and after describing the position of his own physical body, the teacher discusses the favourable conditions under which the subjective equipments of meditation must be brought so that they can hasten the success of the meditator in his contemplation.

"*In a mental attitude of Sannyāsa*" (*Ati-āśrama-sthaḥ*):—Detachment of mind, from the sense-objects and the relief from the consequent mental agitations, is true *Sannyāsa*. The mind has got a habit of running itself out into imagined fields of self-indulgence, of roaming about in the fields of remembered joys of the past in an inherent anxiety to re-live them. To detach the mind from these two perversions is indicated by the term *Sannyāsa*.

"*Having controlled all the senses*" (*Sakal-indriyāṇi-nirudhya*):—Even when a student of meditation selects a quiet place and, even in spite of his spirit of *Sannyāsa*, it is true that the stimuli of the world outside can enter through the sense-organs and build up an agitation in his bosom. A smell or a sound is sometimes more than sufficient to bring into the mind a flood of associated ideas and set the mind wool-gathering into a widening circle of thought-wanderings. It is necessary, therefore, that all the sense-organs, which are inlets for the stimuli to reach the bosom, are completely shut.

Saluting one's own teacher mentally with reverence (*Sva-gurum-praṇamya*):—Mind has got tremendous dynamism. Its energies are stupendous. Ordinarily, its energies are spent up by its profitless wanderings. When all possible wanderings are

* For more details refer *Svāmījī-s* book : Meditation and Life.

blocked, the energies of the mind, which would have otherwise spent, are conserved. The conserved energy multiplies itself, and thus an irresistible column of mental force is dammed up within. The human will, however strong it may be, cannot hold this energy beyond a certain level. The very creative-force of the mind, then shatters the will, and madly runs out into the sensuous world. Such an outburst of mental vitality brings about the fall of a man of self-control.

The river waters held in a dam must find a useful outlet, or else, if the river be perennial, ever alive it will overflow the dam and perhaps, the surge of waters may pull down the dam. But if the waters of the dam are guided through right channels it can irrigate miles of fields all around. Similarly, mental energies conserved in one's own bosom cannot be held idle therein because the source of vitality is a perennial living one. The technique of meditation would have been incomplete if it had only expressed the self-control-aspect of it. Here the teacher is giving us the positive method of intelligently re-directing the conserved energies to an Altar, by doing which the mind itself becomes more quiet, pliable and meditation-worthy.

The instruction is clear. Before meditation, the student is required to bring his prepared mind to the feet of his teacher in an attitude of reverence. If the heart can only love and serve, the head can only judge and respect; but when the head and the heart are brought together, the emotions of love and the spirit of service meet the power of judgement and the sense of respect. They all fuse together to become a rare alloy called "reverence." The attitude of reverence is constituted of both respect and love. When we can come to love that which we respect, or when we feel respect for the very altar of our love, this sacred confluence, this complete attitude is called "reverence."

When a mind is in this attitude of reverence, it becomes to an extent plastic, and we can mould that mind, at this juncture, into any shape that we may choose. At the seat of our meditation, to complete the process of perfecting ourselves, it is neccessary that we must being our mind to this plastic condition.

All that we have, so far, discussed are instructions on how to prepare ourselves before the launching; hereafter the teacher indicates what exactly we must do with such a prepared mind-intellect equipment.

Within the lotus of the heart (*Hṛt-puṇḍrīkam*)—Heart, in philosophy is not the biological organ that pumps the blood to feed the circulatory system. In philosophy and literature, "heart" stands for "the nobler emotions in man that make him human." That arena in the human mind, from where the noble urges of love, kindness, mercy, forgiveness, tolerance, etc., flow out, is called the "heart." Therefore, *within the lotus of the heart* means in a bosom that cherishes these virtues and so, to a large extent, peaceful and serene, contented and fulfilled.

We are thus instructed to meditate in the heart-cave upon (*Brahman*) "the Untainted, the Pure, the Clear and the Grief-less."

In every science the scientist will have to employ a vocabulary of his own and coin new terms to indicate and express novel ideas and rare experiences. The Infinite Consciousness that lies beyond the body, mind and intellect, which "expresses" through these equipments as perceiver, feeler and thinker cannot be expressed or defined in terms of a language which is conceived or constructed only to express all our transactions in the world of objects, feelings and thoughts. But at the same time teachers will have to, if not define, *at least indicate* for us that *state of Pure Consciousness*.

In the Perfect Self, there are neither the world-of-objects perceived, nor the emotions felt, nor the ideas thought of by us today. Under these circumstances the *Upaniṣadik* Seers had to culture out a special language throbbing with its own imports and suggestions, by which they can successfully indicate at once the direction in which the Truth lies as well as Its transcendental nature.

The Infinite is described as *"Untainted and Pure"* (*Virajam Viśuddham*):—Unconditioned by the appetites of the flesh, the agitations of the mind, and the disturbances of the intellect, *It is the Pure*. When we say that a thing is impure, for example, a glass of water, we mean that there is in it something other than itself; hence it is impure. The Infinite Reality, Non-dual and Homogeneous, contains nothing other than Itself, and hence, it is Ever-Pure. Truth is Immaculate.

It is Clear (*Viśadam*)—The Consciousness that illumines for us clearly our feelings and experiences must be "Clear" (Self-effulgent) when we come to experience It. In the light of the sun, we experience the vision of everything around us, and the sun, who illumines for us everything around cannot himself be darkness. Similarly, the Consciousness that illumines for us all our experiences, cannot himself be an Unknowable, when all experiences cease.

"*It is the Griefless*" (*Viśokam*)—Grief is experienced by us only at the body, mind and intellect levels. Transcending these three equipments we have no other sources of pain or grief, and therefore, the State of God-Consciousness, the Self has been indicated in our scriptures as Griefless. In the positive language, this Griefless State is indicated in many *Upaniṣad-s*, as the Bliss Absolute (*Sat-Cit-Ānanda*).

These four terms, *Untainted, Pure, Clear and Griefless* serve as four distinct arrow-marks, each one separately indicating the one and the same Factor that at once presides over the individual and the cosmic life. In the cave-of-the-heart, an attitude of "reverence," sitting comfortably in a quiet place, the *Upaniṣadik Mantra* commands us to meditate upon this great Self. What exactly is this inner process of meditation and how to contemplate are all being described in the following stanza. Some may meditate upon It as a Formless Ideal; others may meditate upon it through a simple form, an idol, representing the ideal. In either case the realisation is of the same goal.

अचिन्त्यमव्यक्तमनन्तरूपं
शिवं प्रशान्तममृतं ब्रह्मयोनिम् ।
तथाऽऽदिमध्यान्तविहीनमेकं
विभुं चिदानन्दमरूपमद्भुतम् ॥ ६ ॥

Acintyam-avyaktam-ananta-rūpaṁ
śivaṁ praśāntam-amṛtaṁ brahma-yonim,
tathā-''di-madhyānta-vihīnam-ekaṁ
vibhuṁ cid-ānandam-arūpam-adbhutam.

अचिन्त्यम् *acintyam* = unthinkable, अव्यक्तम् *avyaktam* = unmanifest; अनन्त-रूपम् *ananta-rūpam* = posessed of endless forms; शिवम् *śivam* = ever-auspicious; प्रशान्तम् *praśāntam*= peaceful; अमृतम् *amṛtam* = immortal; ब्रह्म-योनिम् *brahma-yonim* = the origin of *Brahmadeva*—the Creator; तथा *tathā* = also; आदि-मध्य-अन्त-विहीनम् *ādi-madhya-anta-vihīnam* = without a begining, a middle and an end; एकम् *ekam* =the only one; विभुम् *vibhum* = all-pervading; चिदानन्दम् *cid-ānandam* = the Knowledge-Bliss; अरूपम् *arūpam* = formless; अद्भुतम् *adbhutam* = wonderful.

6. *The Unthinkable, the Unmanifest, the One of endless forms, the Ever-auspicious, the Peaceful, the Immortal, the Origin of the very Creator, the One without a beginning, a middle and an end, the only One, the All-pervading, the Knowledge-Bliss, the Formless, and the wonderful.*

Here, in these thirteen terms, the Eternal Truth, the Self, has been indicated. These terms are given for the purpose of contemplation in the "Cave-of-the-heart." So much so, this *Mantra* is to be understood as complementary to the idea already expressed in the previous one. Each one of these thirteen terms has got its own philosophical implications. To contemplate upon them is to ultimately realise That which all of them together indicate.

Consciousness which is Infinite and Eternal is the Self in each individual. It is the substratum from which all forms have emerged out, are sustained by and into which all forms ultimately disappear. Just as the ocean is the substratum from which the waves and the wavelets, ripples and bubbles are all emerging out, and into which all ultimately sink themselves to become the ocean; so too in life, the Supreme Consciousness is the one Eternal core around which the matter-vehicles ripple out to form the universe. The Infinite Subject is the theme of meditation.

Being thus the very subject in us, the very vitality behind the intellect, that gives us its faculty of intelligence, it cannot become an object of intellectual understanding. To negate all misconceptions that the Supreme Truth is an object of perception, emotion or thought, we are told that it is "unthinkable." In order to be an object of perception it must be manifested when it can be perceived. Since it is not an object perceivable, it is unmanifest. It is the very Subject that perceives all objects. Naturally it is indicated by the term *Unmanifest*.

At the same time, though Unmanifest, all manifestations are nothing but Its own expressions. The ocean is not seen as such among the waves, nor gold among the ornaments; at the same time all ornaments are expressions of gold, all waves are expressions of the ocean. Similarly, the Self as such has manifested to become the objects of perception and, therefore, all manifestations in the pluralistic world, experienced by us, are expressions of the very same Consciousness: hence it is indicated in the *Mantra* here as "*the One, of endless forms*."

Sorrow is inauspicious. Miseries and tragedies, dis-appointments and dis-satisfactions, are all experiences gained by us through the instruments of the body, mind and intellect. Since the Self is that which transcends all equipments of experiences, there, in the Self, while an individual is experiencing the God-consciousness, there cannot be any of these miseries experienced while in the body. And therefore, this

State of Perfection is indicated in the *Upaniṣadik* lore as the *Ever-auspicious* (*Śivam*).

All agitations are doled out for us, in our everyday life, through the disturbances of the thoughts in us. Thoughts in their disturbance create the equipments of emotion and understanding called "mind" and "intellect." Since the Truth is that which functions through the intellect, It transcends both these instruments, and therefore, none of the disturbances and agitations, which are of the nature of these vehicles can ever contaminate the Self. Beyond the source of all disturbances, the *Ātman* is ever supremely peaceful.

Decay or death is mortality. Finitude expresses itself in change. Change from one condition to another is not only the birth of a new condition, but it is also the death of its previous condition. A chain of unending changes is the destiny of the world-of-matter. This experience of continuous mortality is the lot of the ego, when it conceives its world through its own changing restless vehicles of the body, mind and intellect. In the Self, while identifying with the Self, viewed from the Self, the vehicles are no more to give us the apparent delusion of a pluralistic world that surges in its continuous process of change. This changeless constant experience of the Infinite beatitude is pointed out here by the subtle term *Immortal*.

The world is the sum-total of perceptions, emotions and thoughts of all bodies, minds and intellects in the universe. Naturally, therefore, that total creative urge in the Infinite, expressing Itself out according to the total available tendencies and inclinations (*Vāsanā-s*) is the very Creator of the universe. Creative urge, that is already there in the Omnipotent Truth, when dynamised by Truth, is expressed as the Creator. This, the very womb from which the Creative Power has risen, is but the Truth alone, and hence the Supreme is indicated here as the *Origin of the very Creator*.

"The One without a beginning a middle or an end" (*Ādi-madhya-anta-vihīnam-ekam*)—That which is limited by time

alone can have a beginning, an end, and therefore, a middle. In the flood of time alone there are the concepts of the past, future and the mingling of the two, called the present. Time itself is a concept of the intellect. In deep sleep, swooning, or when under choloform, when the human intellect is blanketed off and rendered unserviceable temporarily, and as long as it is not functioning, there is no concept of time for the individual. When the individual emerges from sleep, immediately the concept of time asserts itself. The Self is experienced when the intellect is transcended; naturally, in that experience of the Self, the "concept of time" is also by-passed. Hence the Supreme is indicated by the term "that which has neither a beginning, nor a middle, nor an end," meaning that which is "not conditioned by time."

That which is thus the very Origin of the Creator—meaning that which existed even before the Creator was born to create the pluralistic world, and that which is unconditioned by time and place must necessarily be *One Eternal Factor* which is All-pervading and Formless. That which is *One* must necessarily be all-pervading because if it is not pervading everywhere, it should imply the existence of something other than itself, which is to limit it. Philosophically viewed, that which is One-without-a-second must necessarily be All-pervading. That which is All-pervading cannot have a form because form denotes limitations. The unlimited is the formless. In terms of our intellect, It is inconceivable and therefore, the best we can say is that It is *wonderful*.

Also it is a fact that when wonder or amazement strikes us, temporarily our intellect and mind halt, benumbed by the very experience. Through meditation when the man transcends his own intellect he comes to the same experience, wherein his mind and intellect no more function and, therefore, very often the *Ṛṣī*-s indicate the Truth experience in terms of the psychological condition experienced by us when we are struck with extreme wonder.

The above thirteen terms, which we have tried to individually treat in the discourse, together in their sum-total suggest a deep inner realm-of-experience which is the theme for contemplation. Intellectually to conceive all these ideas and emotionally to come to feel these, and thus heave together to reach and experience it, constitutes meditation. Thus *meditation* is explained here, which is indeed a full explanation of the instructions given in the previous stanza that in the heart cave the meditator must contemplate upon the "Untainted, Pure, Clear, Griefless."

In order to meditate thus upon the Formless Infinite, a certain amount of subtlety of the intellect is to be developed. Majority of us have not got that amount of self-mastery and contemplative dynamism now in our nature, and even those who are practitioners of meditation must get themselves prepared for their meditative flights. The immatured is rendered mature for meditation and the unprepared is prepared for the flight in contemplation, by a relatively simple process of worship and concentration upon a symbol of the Formless Absolute. This preparatory technique is called worship (*Upāsanā*). This process is explained in the following stanza.

उमासहायं परमेश्वरं प्रभुं
त्रिलोचनं नीलकण्ठं प्रशान्तम् ।
ध्यात्वा मुनिर्गच्छति भूतयोनिं
समस्तसाक्षिं तमसः परस्तात् ॥ ७ ॥

Umā-sahāyaṁ parameśvaraṁ prabhuṁ
tri-locanaṁ nīla-kaṇṭhaṁ praśāntam,
dhyātvā munir-gacchati bhūta-yoniṁ
samasta-sākṣiṁ tamasaḥ parastāt.

उमा-सहायम् *umā-sahāym* = consorted with *Umā*; परमेश्वरम् *parameśvaram* = *Paramśvara*, the Highest Lord; प्रभुम् *prabhum* = Lord, all-powerful; त्रिलोचनम् *tri-locanam* = three-eyed; नील-कण्ठम

nīla-kaṇṭham = Blue-necked; प्रशान्तम् *praśāntam* = the ever-tranquil; ध्यात्वा *dhyātvā* = by meditating upon; मुनिः *muniḥ* = man of reflection; गच्छति *gacchati* = reaches, (lit. goes); भूत-योनिम् *bhūta-yonim* = the Source of all the manifested world; समस्त-साक्षिम् *samasta-sākṣim* = the Witness of all; तमसः *tamasaḥ* = from darkness; परस्तात् *parastāt* = beyond.

7. *By meditating upon Lord* Parameśvara *consorted by mother* Umā, *the Highest Lord, the all-powerful, the three-eyed, the blue-necked and the ever-tranquil, a true man of reflection reaches Him, who is the Source of all the manifested world, the Witness-of-all, and who is beyond all darkness.*

If the former was a description of meditation upon the Formless, here we have a "Form-full meditation." In symbol worship, the meditator finds it relatively easy to place his entire attention upon the idol and when his wandering mind is thus brought to rest upon the idol, the intellect springs forth to contemplate and realise the ideal that the idol represents. This is the theory behind all symbol worship, be it a *Śivaliṅga* or a *Śālagrāma*, be it a Cross or a Crescent, be it a Pagoda or a Pyramid.

It is significant that in the stanza, Lord *Parameśvara* along with his consort is meditated upon by a diligent seeker who is "a man of reflection" (*Muni*). A simple, emotional approach to the symbol, however intense and devoted it may be, is not sufficient, for, only a part of our personality is brought into play in such worship. Emotion alone is not everything. It represents only the heart-aspect in man. The intellectual nature in him also needs integration. Therefore, the students must contemplate upon the suggestive picture of the Lord and His Consort.

Matter itself is inert. It constitutes the vehicles of expression of the Spirit. The matter-vehicles that constitute the world-forms together make the *Prakṛti*; and the vitalising Spirit behind them all, the principle that expresses through the inert matter vehicles (*Prakṛti*), is called the *Puruṣa*. This *Puruṣa* wedded to *Prakṛti* is the manifested expression of the entire pluralistic world-of-objects. *Puruṣa* expresses His vitality and manifests His Omnipotency without, through the vehicles of expression, the *Prakṛti*. And the vehicles of expression can never express themselves without being blessed by the *Puruṣa*.

The *Prakṛti* and *Puruṣa* wedded together, maintain among themselves, a relationship similar to that of a flutist and his flute, or a writer and his pen. Neither the pen contains poetry nor the flute has music. And, the poet and the musician, doubtless do throb with poetry and music, but they cannot express them without the appropriate instruments. The Flute of Matter is thrilled by the Spirit, and there issues out the cadence of life, thundering forth its varied songs of joys and sorrows. These concepts of *Prakṛti* and *Puruṣa* are symbolised here as *Umā* and *Parameśvara*—*Umā* is an instrument for *Parameśvara* to express Himself.

Parameśvara is the Lord and the Master (*Prabhu*) in each individual bosom. Our physical, mental and intellectual experiences are not at all possible without the Presence of Life in us. The spark of Life, the Spirit, thrills the vehicles enabling us to live and gain our various experiences. He in whose presence all departments of activities function, in whose absence all activities get closed down, is the proprietor or master of any given institution. The Self, the presiding Life in us, is the Divine Master (*Prabhu*) who, by His mere presence, thrills the instruments to continue their activities rhythmically: the activities of perception, feeling and thought.

This *Parameśvara* is described in the *Śiva Purāṇa* as three-eyed.* To the hasty readers, who recognise not the Law of Symbolism, carrying as they do, with them the traditional belief of some cheap creed and religion, there will be an inclination to dismiss all such descriptions like this, as

* The three eyes i. e. *Tri-cakṣu* represent *Prem*, *Jñāna* and *Nyāya;* while two eyes observe *Dvaita,* the third one looks up to *Advaita.*---*Ed.*

mythological absurdities. In fact, we have in India no mythology at all. We have only "mystic symbolism."

Self, the Pure Consciousness not only illumines, through the vehicles, the world as perceived by us in our present state of Consciousness, but also has a vision of Its own, which can be experienced by us only when we transcend the vehicles. Lord *Śiva* is thus pictured as having not only the fleshy eyes of the mortal, but also a "third eye" on His forehead—the Eye of Intuition, the Vision of Pure Knowledge. It is described in *Śiva Purāṇa* that in His ecstasy of joy, dancing in His meditation seat, when he opens his third-eye, the entire world of Names and Forms around Him gets burnt out. This is one of the incomparable mystic pictures that signify the mighty one, who, on waking up to the God Consciousness, transcends the limited vision of the world of Names and Forms, and comes to live the Universal Oneness.

The blue-necked (*Nīla-kaṇṭha*):—In the glorious story of Lord *Śiva*, it is described how in the preparation of Nectar (*Amṛta*) the Gods and the Demons churned the milky ocean with the mountain *Maṁdara* as the churning rod and the self-volunteered *Vāsuki* (one of the foremost eight serpent-kings) as the churning rope.

Pulled forward and backward by the mighty teams of the gods and the demons the churning went on, when very many wonders and things glorious emerged out, but the determined crowd continued the process of churning. Just before they reached the great achievement, *Vāsuki* (the *Naga-rājā*) exhausted and tired by the strain and stress, vomitted its terrible poison. Frightened by this calamity, the helpless demons cried out for protection to Lord *Śiva*. He came and received the flowing lava of poison, in his palm. It was so terrible that it could be neither thrown up nor poured down because it would destroy everything wonderful. Naturally, therefore, the Lord drank it, as if, in a spirit of self-sacrifice for the sake of His devotees. *Umā*, seeing the desperate act of Her Consort, pressed

His throat not allowing the poison to go down. Thus it got held up in the neck, turning its colour into blue.

The story as it stands looks as fantastic as it is crude, but when the symbolism is understood one will appreciate the great wisdom of the *Ṛṣī-s* in packing up an entire philosophy in this unforgettable piece of literature.

Subjectively, in each of us when the churning is done in our purified *Sāttvik* mind (the milky ocean), with the intellect (*Maṁdara*) that supports the mind, and the rope of ego (serpent-king *Vāsuki*) by the lower (*asurā*-s) and the higher (*Devā*-s) in us, meditation starts. In the early stages of this meditation (churning) many tempting profits (*Siddhī-s*) emerge out but if the churning is continued, a time would come when, just before the experiences of immortality (*Amṛta*), the ego (*Vāsuki*) must vomit out its entire subconscious and unconscious *Vāsanā-s* (poison). This great "poison of ignorance" cannot be totally eliminated until Wisdom (*Jñānam*) dawns. This ignorance can only be held in the neck—indicating a point away from and between the head and the heart. Ego and ego-centric desires should not be allowed to poison either the head or heart of the meditator at this moment, and naturally, when the churning continues the Supreme experience is unfolded and the goal is gained.

Thus, the cause of agitations and disturbances is one's identification with the matter vehicles and the Supreme Spirit gets identified with the body, mind and intellect, there is the expression of the ego. Ego is, and it must necessarily be, always in a state of restlessness and discontentment. When the matter vehicles are transcended, when the *Puruṣa* is no more expressing through the *Prakṛti*, the Supreme State is experienced which is, and should be, always, ever-peaceful: *Praśāntam*.

When all these symbolic details are reflected upon, the men of reflection (*Muni*) must needfully reach the Source of all the manifested world (*Bhūta-yoni*)*—the Eternal Self.

* *Bhavanti-iti-Bhūtāni—Whosoever is born or has manifested comes under the category of Bhūta.---Ed.*

The Absolute in Its Perfection has nothing to achieve in order to complete Its happiness. But when It expresses through matter, it looks as if the Spirit is struggling through matter for happiness. The great seers of the *Upaniṣad-s* declare that the Spirit is only a mere Witness of everything (*Samasta Sākṣim*). A witness is he who comprehends an incident without himself having any personal interest in it; nor does he get himself involved in the incident. Thus relationship between the Absolute Spirit and the finite matter has been described by *Śrī Śaṅkarācārya* (in *Ātma bodha* Stanza-20) with a beautiful analogy. He compares this relationship within our bosom, with that of the sun and the world of activities. When the sun rises, our intelllect wakes up and drawing its nature and nourishment, vitality and strength from the sun, gets activised in the world, each one pursuing his own activities ordered by his past inclinations. If the sun were not there, all activities would cease; but the sun himself is not directly responsible for the what and the how of each individual's activity. Similarly the Spirit, the Self, is the Witness of all and the vehicles of matter draw their capacities and capabilities from the warmth of life and each one acts according to one's own inclinations and pursues one's own purposes.

Beyond all darkness, this inner experience is extremely clear and supremely subjective. There is no doubt in the individual regarding the nature and reality of this experience. Just as a dreamer no more doubts, when he once wakes up, about the nature and reality of the waking world, so too an ego-centric individual, when he comes to the plane of God-Consciousness, his experience is so all-consuming that there is no doubt left in him as to the reality of his present experience.

Complete and total realisation is possible. This is the assertion of all the *Vedāntik* Seers.

स ब्रह्मा स शिवः सेन्द्रः सोऽक्षरः परमः स्वराट् ।
स एव विष्णुः स प्राणः स कालोऽग्निः स चन्द्रमाः ॥ ८ ॥

Sa brahmā sa śivaḥ sendraḥ
so-'kṣaraḥ paramaḥ svarāṭ,
sa eva viṣṇuḥ sa prāṇaḥ
sa kālo-'gniḥ sa candramāḥ.

सः *saḥ* = He; ब्रह्मा *brahmā* = *Brahmadeva*; सः *saḥ* = he; शिवः *śivaḥ* = *Śiva*; सः *saḥ* = he; इन्द्रः *indraḥ* = *Indra*; सः *saḥ* = he; अक्षरः *akṣaraḥ* = the immutable; परमः *paramaḥ* = supreme; स्वराट् *svarāṭ* = self-luminous; सः *saḥ* = he; एव *eva* = alone; विष्णुः *viṣṇuḥ* = *Viṣṇu*; सः *saḥ* = he; प्राणः *prāṇaḥ* = *prāṇa*; सः *saḥ* = he; कालः *kālaḥ* = time; अग्निः *agniḥ* = fire; सः *saḥ* = he; चन्द्रमाः *candramāḥ* = moon.

8. *He is* Brahmā; *He is* Śiva, *He is* Indra, *He is the Immutable, the Supreme, the Self-luminous. He alone is* Viṣṇu, *He is* Prāṇa, *He is Time and Fire. He is the Moon.*

The experience of the previous stanza arising out of devoted concentration upon Lord *Parameśvara* is the experience of the Supreme. That which is experienced through worship of the form-symbol (*Saguṇopāsanā*) is ultimately of the Immutable Transcendental Reality. All idols, though different in form and conceived in different attitudes, symbolise but the One Supreme Consciousness, which in Its real nature transcends all of them. No idol is in itself the ideal, the ideal is indicated by the representing idol. Since the Truth is one, whatever be the symbol taken up for prayer and worship by a particular individual, it also must symbolise this Great Reality. All idols when meditated upon must necessarily give but one and the same inner experience. An individual can be pointed out with different qualities, capacities, possessions or relationships. And yet, the individual indicated by all these terms will necessarily be one and the same.*

---

* Son of *Daśaratha*, husband of *Sītā*, brother of *Lakṣamaṇa*, King of *Ayodhyā*, destroyer of *Rāvaṇa*, Lord of *Haṇumāna*, Lord of the Bow—all are but *Śrī Rāmacandra* Himself.

Based upon this principle of our everyday experiences, the great *Parameṣṭhi*, the teacher of the *Kaivalyopaniṣad*, asserts that the Great Self within us Itself is *Brahmā, Śiva, Indra, Viṣṇu, Prāṇa*, Time, Fire, Moon etc. It is to be noted that the above enumerated list indicates the important deities worshipped in the *Vedik* period—just the same way as in our times we have got the *Paurāṇik* deities whom we invoke in our daily religious functions. All of them are symbolising the One and the same glorious Truth.

Immutable (*Akṣara*) : That which undergoes change is the perishable finite world of matter. Therefore, the changeless eternal Truth is generally indicated as the Immutable, the Imperishable. Subjectively it also indicates that *Ātman*, the Self, is something other than the equipments of experience which we all know in our experiences to be ever changing and mutable.

Supreme (*paramam*) : When we analyse the known realm of matter, we find the body (*Annamaya*) is ruled by the physiological function-layer (*Prāṇamaya*) in us, which in its turn is ordered by the condition of our mind (*Manomaya*). The dance of emotions and feelings are to the beat of intellectual thoughts (*Vijñānamaya*), which in turn are ordered by the *Vāsanā-s* (*Ānandamaya*). Thus, in one's own quest in oneself for the Ultimate Reality, in fact, one comes to detect subtler and subtler realms within, which order the grosser and outer layers of matter. When the *Śāstrā-s* tell us that all these, including the *Vāsanā-s* are illumined by the Supreme Consciousness, there still lingers a doubt in us as to whether there is yet another subtle entity behind the *Ātman*. To deny that there can be anything subtler than the Self, and to assert that the Self is the Subtlest of Subtle, the Ultimate Reality is declared here to be the Supreme (*Paramam*)

Self-luminous (*Sva-rāṭ*)—There is a set of triple words in *Saṁskṛta* indicating the might and glory of the Macrocosm Life expressing through the entire world of gross forms and names in its totality is called *Vi-rāṭ*. The Supreme expressing through the "Total mind and intellect," prompted by the "total-

Vāsanā-s," is called '*Sam-rāṭ.*' And the Infinite Consciousness, the One non-dual Reality, which functions through every name and form, moving and unmoving, existent and non-existent, in Its own Immaculate nature, is termed as *Sva-rāṭ*. Therefore, *Sva-rāṭ* is the "Self-luminous" since it has no objects to illumine other than Itself.

स एव सर्वं यद् भूतं यच्च भव्यं सनातनम् ।
ज्ञात्वा तं मृत्युमत्येति नान्यः पन्था विमुक्तये ॥ ९ ॥

Sa eva sarvaṁ yad bhūtaṁ
yacca bhavyaṁ sanātanam,
jñātvā taṁ mṛtyum-atyeti
nānyaḥ panthā vimuktaye.

सः *saḥ* = he; एव *eva* = alone; सर्वम् *sarvam* = all; यद् *yad* = which; भूतम् *bhūtam* = was; यत् *yat* = which; च *ca* = and; भव्यम् *bhavyam* = will be; सनातनम् *sanātanam* = Eternal; ज्ञात्वा *jñātvā* = Knowing; तम् *tam* = him; मृत्युम् *mṛtyum* = death; अत्येति *atyeti* = crosses; न *na* = not; अन्यः *anyaḥ* = other; पन्थाः *panthāḥ* = path; विमुक्तये *vimuktaye* = for liberation.

9. *He alone is all that was, and all that will be, the Eternal; knowing Him, one goes beyond the sting of death; there is no other way to reach complete freedom.*

Just as, in the dream the one waking mind itself becomes the varieties of objects and beings in the dream; so too, it is this Transcendental Consciousness behind, that has become the pluralistic world at all periods of time. All that was in the past (*Bhūtam*), and all that will be in the future (*Bhavyam*) is nothing but the expressions of Him, the One Eternal (*Sanātana*) Reality, Lord *Parameśvara.*

"*Having known*" (*Jñātvā*):—To know this is the Highest Knowledge. Here 'Knowing' is not a mere intellectual appreciation but a spiritual apprehension, whereby the seeker knows the Truth in his own deep and vivid subjective experience; it must be known in a living spiritual apprehension.

One who has thus awakened to the *Parameśvara*-Consciousness becomes hismelf the *Nīlakānṭha*, and since the Lord *Trilocana* is Immortal, such a seeker also goes beyond death. We have already explained the term "Immortality' as a state of experience which never changes or waves.

"There is no other way to complete freedom" (*Nānya Panthāḥ Vimuktaye*):—Ordinarily a student might feel that this is a very difficult path and, therefore, would expect the teacher to give him something more ready-to-do technique. To deny that there is no short cut to Perfection and that this alone is the method, the *Upaniṣad-s* very often have to make such total assertions.

To rise above our identification with mind and intellect by a conscious contemplative flight is the only method of awakening into the Truth and reaching the Higher Consciousness. Until this Seat of Truth is entered into and lived in our own subjective experience, we cannot rise above the thraldom-of-matter, which is the source of all our suffering today.

सर्वभूतस्थमात्मानं सर्वभूतानि चात्मनि ।
सम्पश्यन् ब्रह्म परमं याति नान्येन हेतुना ॥ १० ॥

Sarva-bhūta-stham-ātmānaṁ sarva-bhūtāni cātmani,
sampaśyan brahma paramaṁ yāti nānyena hetunā.

सर्व-भूत-स्थम् *sarva-bhūta-stham* = staying in all beings; आत्मानम् *ātmānam* = Self; सर्व-भूतानि *sarva-bhūtāni* = all beings; च *ca* = and; आत्मनि *ātmani* = in Self; सम्पश्यन् *sampaśyan* = experiencing; ब्रह्म *brahma* = *Brahman*; परमम् *paramam* = Highest; याति *yāti* = attains (lit. goes); न *na* = not; अन्येन *anyena* = by other; हेतुना *hetunā* = means.

10. *Experiencing one's own Self in all beings and all beings in the Self, one attains the Highest Brahman—and not by any other means.*

It was already said by the teacher in the very opening stanza of the *Upaniṣad* that neither by *Karma* (*Sakāma*) nor through dependants (progeny), nor by wealth or possessions can we reach the Highest Immutable Reality. The same idea is emphasised here. We can gain this Truth neither by sincere self-effort in the outer world (*karmaṇā*), nor by the help of those who are our well-wishers (*Prajayā*), nor by all our highly developed subjective faculties or our acquired objective possessions (*dhanena*). Truth is gained only in the intimate moment of subjective experience of it. What then is the moment of this awakening, the experience of *Nirvāṇa*?

Just as on awakening from a dream we realise that all the objects that we saw in dream were nothing but the expressions of our own mind; so too, one who is experiencing the Self realises that the entire world-of-objects, that he had been seeing before, have all merged back into the Self. And thereafter, when a man-of-realisation looks out into the world, no doubt, he perceives the world of plurality but he also experiences the play of same Self in and through each one of them.

Thus, if in meditation he sees the world of perfections, emotions and thoughts dissolving themselves to become one mass of Consciousness, the Self, he, on waking from the Self, in all his empirical experiences, does not totally forget or lose sight of the experienced Reality, but readily detects at all times the play of the One Consciousness in and through the multiple forms. The first line of this stanza we read in the *Bhagavad Gītā* (VI-29) where oneness of the macrocosm and the microcosm is meant.

This total experience of the Self, as full within and without is indicated here by the term *Sampaśyan*. Such an individual entity who has liquidated his ego-centric individuality is the one who reaches the portals of Truth and fully experiences It.

Here also the teacher asserts for the benefit of the student that this alone is the only means by which the Supreme can be experienced—there is no other means (*Na anyena hetunā*).

आत्मानमरणिं कृत्वा प्रणवं चोत्तरारणिं ।
ज्ञाननिर्मथनाभ्यासात् पाशं दहति पण्डितः ॥ ११ ॥

Ātmānam-araṇiṁ kṛtvā praṇavaṁ cottarāraṇiṁ,
jñāna-nirmathanā-bhyāsāt pāśaṁ dahati paṇḍitaḥ.

आत्मानम् *ātmānam* = individual Self; अरणिम् *araṇim* = a piece of firewood; कृत्वा *kṛtvā* = making; प्रणवम् *praṇavam* = *Oṁkāra, Brahman*; च *ca* = and; उत्तर-अरणिम् *uttara-araṇim* = upper piece of firewood; ज्ञान-निर्मथन-अभ्यासात् *jñāna-nirmathana-abhyāsāt* = through the practice of churning of knowledge; पाशम् *pāśam* = bondage; दहति *dahati* = burns; पण्डितः *paṇḍitaḥ* = wise.

11. *Making the ego the "lower* Araṇi*" and* Oṁ *the "upper* Araṇi,*" through the practice of repeated churning of Knowledge* "Jñāna nirmathana abhyāsa,*" a wise man burns up all the chords of his bondage.*

In case the seeker has no such experience of the Divine Presence, at once in himself and in all names and forms around him, how is he to get it? This is answered here in this *mantra.*

Life expressed through the body, mind and intellect becomes the perceiver, feeler, thinker entity. This is the ego-centric individuality in each one of us which lives through the imperfections of the body, the agitations of the mind and the restless cravings of the intellect. Spirit manifested through mattter is the ego (*Jīva*); the *Jīva* depends upon the conditions of the matter vehicles around it.

This *Jīva* is to meditate upon the nature of the Infinite Truth as described earlier,* or through meditation upon *Parameśvara*, who represents this Great Self, the individual is to

* Ibid Stanza-5.

get prepared for the meditation-flight. By this process the *Jīva* gets detached from the encumbrances of its mind-intellect and thereby comes to recognise its essential nature as the *Brahman*. *Praṇava* is the sound symbol of *Brahman*, the Supreme Reality.

This process of meditation is described here in a metaphor borrowed from the "churning of fire" in the *Vedik* ritualism of *Yajñā-s* and *Yāgā-s*. In the bygone days, the sacred altar for ritualism was lit up with fire freshly invoked by the continuous rubbing of two pieces of wood. This was accomplished through a technical process known as '*churning up of the fire*.' Between two cups, scooped in wooden blocks, a cylindrical rod of wood is fixed perpendicular and the rod is rotated by a piece of rope exactly as in the process of churning butter in our villages. When the perpendicular wooden rod is churned between the pressed upper and lower blocks (*Araṇī-s*), due to friction, first a piece of cotton catches fire and from it when properly tended, fire can be gained and this fire sets the arranged fuel-pile in the "sacred trough" (*Kuṇḍa*) ablaze. This is a religious function very often witnessed by all the seekers of the *Upaniṣad-s*.

Using this metaphor to explain what happens in the inner life of the seekers, it is said the "lower block" is the ego-attitude in us; the "upper block" is the *Praṇava*, meaning *Oṁ*, which is the sound-symbol of the Infinite Life, the Self-Divine. When these two are connected together and the lower-Self is uplifted to the glowing nature of the Higher Self, through contemplation and steady meditation, the seeker loses his identifications with his outer layer of matter. The Immaculate Divinity in us, bound with matter, lives through the delusory agonies of Imperfections, which is the nature of the ever-changing matter. Even when we intellectually understand our true nature to be absolutely free from matter entanglements, because of our clinging bondages with these equipments, we fail to walk out of the dens of delusion into the outer shining realms of the Universal Reality.

When this practice is undertaken for a sufficiently long time, the *Jīva* comes to experience the higher possibilities in itself and the Fire of Knowledge so kindled in one's own bosom burns down one's chords of shameless bondage with the flesh : *"The wise man burns up the chords of the bondage."*

"Praṇava":—*"Oṁkāra Upāsanā"* is the *"Praṇava-upāsanā."* The sound symbol that stands for the Infinite *Brahman* is *Praṇava.* To meditate upon the nature of *Brahman* as indicated by the *"Praṇava"* is the method of lifting ourselves slowly from the ego-centric misconception of our life into that true nature of the Reality.

The process of contemplating upon the nature of the Self as our own nature (*Ahaṅkāra-upāsanā*) is the "churning of Knowledge," (*Jñāna Manthana*) indicated in the *mantra.* How this is done is the contents of the following pairs of stanzas.

It is very well-known that matter is inert. Though the body, mind and intellect are composed of matter, we are not insentient, inert things, but in our own experience we are sentient and dynamic creatures. Thus it is evidently clear that Consciousness or Spirit expressing through matter is the manifested entity in each one of us. To analyse the subjective experience of life in each one of us, as we pass from one State of Consciousness into another, is the most direct method of detecting and apprehending the Self. This is being done by the self-investigation of the seeker himself playing as the waker, dreamer and deep-sleeper in himself.

स एव माया परिमोहितात्मा
शरीरमास्थाय करोति सर्वम् ।
स्त्र्यन्नपानादिविचित्रभोगैः
स एव जाग्रत्परितृप्तिमेति ॥ १२ ॥

Sa eva māyā parimohitātmā
śarīram-āsthāya karoti sarvam,
stry-anna-pānādi-vicitra-bhogaiḥ
sa eva jāgrat-pari-tṛptim-eti.

स *sa*= He; एव *eva* = alone; माया परिमोहित आत्मा *māyā parimohita-ātmā* = Self deluded by *Māyā*; शरीरम् *śarīram* = body; आस्थाय *āsthāya* = staying; करोति *karoti* = does; सर्वम् *sarvam* = all; स्त्रि-अन्न-पान-आदि-विचित्र-भोगैः *stri-anna-pāna-ādi-vicitra-bhogaiḥ* = through the varied objects of enjoyment such as woman, food, wine, etc.; स *sa* = he; एव *eva* = alone; जाग्रत् *jāgrat* = waking; परितृप्तिम् *paritṛptim* = full gratification; एति *eti* = goes, reaches.

12. *The Self, deluded by* Māyā, *is he who identifying with the body does all actions (all perceptions, feelings and thoughts). In the waking state it is he (this* Jīva), *who reaches full gratification through the varied objects of enjoyment such as woman, food, wine etc.*

"*Self deluded by Māyā*" (*Māyā Parimohita ātmā*):—The tendencies and impressions left behind by the marching thoughts and actions upon the fields of the intellect together constitute *Māyā* or ignorance. These tendencies or *Vāsanā-s* gurgle forth as desires and wishes, and they order and control the type of thoughts and their direction of flow in the human personality. The mind-intellect which is the thought-flow is caused by the *Vāsanā-s*, and the mind-intellect equipment decides in its turn the type of body and the nature of the environments in which it must come to function. Thus the *Vāsanā-s* constitute the Causal Body (*Avidyā*) which in its turn projects the subtle body (Mind and intellect), who in their nature and quality order the gross body and the environmental field of activities. This microcosmic Causal Body (*Avidyā*) in its macrocosmic dignity is termed as *Māyā*.

The Supreme Consciousness functioning through "*Avidyā*" (*Māyā*) is the individual "*Jīva.*"

Naturally, in order to express and fulfil its thoughts and desires it assumes a physical body and ordered by its own *Vāsanā-s* acts differently. Due to the compelling urgencies of the existing *Vāsanā-s* the Pure Immaculate Nature of Its own Divinity is lost sight of by the Self, and It becomes completely extrovert in nature, striving and straining through the body to eke out its joys from the world of sensuous objects—"Women, food, wine etc." Assured by its intellect it orders different things and arranges and re-arranges them into different patterns so that it may gain its varieties of sense gratifications (*Vicitra-bhogaiḥ*).

Forgetting Its own Infinite Blissful Nature in its identification with Its own *Vāsanā-s*, the Self becomes, as though, limited and striving through the physical body to contact the world-of-objects, and through sense gratifications it labours to gain a sense of utter satisfaction. This seeker-of-joy, functioning through the body in the world-of-objects, is the "Waker" in each one of us.

When this idea of the waking personality is correctly apprehended as a result of our reflection upon the contents of this stanza the student's attention is turned towards the "Dreamer" personality in himself, in the following stanza :

स्वप्ने स जीवः सुखदुःखभोक्ता
स्वमायया कल्पितजीवलोके ।
सुषुप्तिकाले सकले विलीने
तमोऽभिभूतः सुखरूपमेति ॥ १३ ॥

Svapne sa jīvaḥ sukha-duḥkha-bhoktā
sva-māyayā kalpita-jīvaloke,
suṣupti-kāle sakale vilīne
tamo-'bhibhūtaḥ sukha-rūpam-eti.

स्वप्ने *svapne* = in dream; स *sa* = he; जीवः *jīvaḥ* = individual soul; सुख-दुःख-भोक्ता *sukha-duḥkha-bhoktā* = experiencer of pleasure and pain; स्व-मायया *sva-māyayā* = by his own *Māyā*; कल्पित जीवलोके *kalpita jīvaloke* = in the imagined world; सुषुप्ति काले *suṣupti kāle* = at the time of deep sleep; सकले विलीने *sakale vilīne* = when all is merged; तमः अभिभूतः *tamaḥ-abhibhūtaḥ* = over-powered by ignorance; सुख रूपम् *sukha rūpam* = form of Bliss; एति *eti* = attains.

13. *The very same individualised ego in the "dream-state" experiences its pleasure and pain—in a field of existence created by its own* Māyā *(Misapprehension of Reality). During the "state of profound sleep" when everything is merged (into their causal state), it is overpowered by* Tamas *(non-apprehension) and comes to exist in its form of Bliss.*

Continuing the autobiography of the Spirit as functioning through the external vestures, the teacher in *Kaivalyopaniṣad,* Lord *Brahmā,* the Creator, narrates the formation of the Dreamer and its experiences in the dream-land of its own creation. The Infinite Self when it gathers itself from the "physical body," constituted of the anatomical structures and the physiological functions, and experiences Itself through the "subtle-body," consisting of the mind and intellect, there is the manifestation of the "Dreamer-entity."

So long as one is conscious of one's own body, it is impossible for one to have the "dreamer" personality. Where the body-consciousness has sprung up, there the dream experiences end; "dreamer" is none other than the "waker" who has no more the consciousness of his body—and therefore, not conscious of the field-of-objects interpreted by the body—and the "dreamer" functions at the subtle body, with its own thoughts. The dream-land (*Svapna prapañca*) created by the dreamer's own mind becomes the field of his joys and tragedies for him throughout his dream-condition.

Identifying himself with the world so created, the "dreamer" establishes in himself a subject-object relationship in his dream and comes to experience its joys and sorrows.

"*By its own non-apprehensions*" (*Māyā*):—" Non-apprehension of Reality is the cause for all mis-apprehensions of it." The *ignorance of the post* brings forth the mis-apprehensions of some ghost-like apparitions. The *ignorance of the waking condition* and the consequent non-apprehension of the "waker"- personality gives the mind a freedom to project itself into a thousand varieties of mis-apprehensions. This power in the human mind to veil the Reality, and in its place to project unreal imaginations, which have for the time being a perfect look of reality for the deluded, is called the "power of *Māyā*" (*Māyā śakti*).

Tracing the activities of That which expressed as the "waker" in the waking and as a "dreamer" in the dreaming, the teacher continuous to give us a true picture of the "deep sleeper," who enjoys the dreamless sleep. In the "waker" the Self is functioning through the *gross body*, in the "dreamer" is the same Self expressing through the *subtle body*, and in the "deep sleeper" is the glory of the Self manifested through the *causal body*.

The causal body is constituted of the *Vāsanā-s*. Thoughts are born out of the *Vāsanā-s*; thoughts order the type of emotions of the mind; and the state of the mind orders the texture of one's actions. The type of actions determines the envirnoments and circumstances around the actor. Thus, if the cause of action be emotions, the emotions themselves are ordered by thoughts; therefore, the cause of the thoughts, the very *Vāsanā-s* naturally form the subtlest cause for all manifestations of the Life Eternal in any individual. Hence they form the *causal body* in man.

To be in the *causal body* is to be in the *causal state,* the tree in the seed is in its causal condition. Under favourable circumstances the unmanifested tree in the seed can manifest. But in the seed it is unmanifest and is in the causal condition.

In deep sleep, the Self expresses through the *causal body* and therefore, there is no manifestation of life as thoughts or emotions or actions. This condition of the Self functioning through the *causal body*, when the individuality in us is in its causal condition, is called the deep-sleep state-of-Consciousness.

The manifestations that were familiar for the "waker" and the "dreamer" are no more here in the deep-sleep; these two realms of plurality seem to have got absorbed here into their causal condition.

"Overpowered by Tamas" (*Tamo abhibhūtaḥ*):—The experience of deep-sleep is total non-apprehension of everything, a total "ignorance." This condition is described here as "overpowered by *Tamas*." When a room is plunged in darkness, we have no knowledge of what it contains. Many things of beauty or danger may be there; but so long as these objects lie shrouded under a blanket of darkness, we have no knowledge of them.

In fact to say that it is all darkness is not totally true. It would be perhaps true to say that the individuality (*Jīva*) is in its deep-sleep-state in the "blindening light of Truth" and the intensity of Its effulgence has so utterly benumbed the "sleeper's" grosser awareness that he is rendered utterly blind.

However, the "non-apprehension of Reality" (*Tamas*) cannot yield any quota of positive sorrow, nor can it give even an iota of joy: it is a negative state of impotent neutrality. Since the sorrow breeding plurality of the waking and the dream conditions is not there to persecute the "deep-sleeper," in his empirical experience he has to accept his sleep as a condition of bliss.

Thus, in this stanza and in the previous one, the teacher of the *Upaniṣad* has brought to the acute awareness of the seeker the nature, function and the field of activities of the Self manifested through Its identifications with the gross, the subtle and the causal bodies. Such a clear analysis and close observation in the laboratory of contemplation of the three states of Consciousness* brings the seeker to a state of subjective introvertedness and intelligent self-analysis. If one could do so,

* The Waking, Dream and Deep-sleep states of Consciousness.

without one's mind getting distracted by the world-of-objects outside, that individual will enter into a field of subjective meditation and in himself watch his potential power of contemplation unfolding to its highest efficiency.

पुनश्च जन्मान्तरकर्मयोगात्
स एव जीवः स्वपिति प्रबुद्धः ।
पुरत्रये क्रीडति यश्च जीवः
ततस्तु जातं सकलं विचित्रम् ॥
आधारमानन्दमखण्डबोधं
यस्मिंल्लयं याति पुरत्रयं च ॥ १४ ॥

Punaśca janmāntara-karma-yogāt,
sa eva jīvaḥ svapiti prabuddhaḥ,
pura-traye krīḍati yaśca jīvaḥ
tatastu jātaṁ sakalaṁ vicitram.
ādhāram-ānandam-akhaṇḍa-bhodhaṁ
yasmiṁ-llayaṁ yāti pura-trayaṁ ca.

पुनः *punaḥ* = again; च *ca* = and; जन्म-अन्तर-कर्म-योगात् *janma-antara-karma-yogāt* = due to the deeds done in other lives; सः *saḥ* = he; एव *eva* = alone; जीवः *jīvaḥ* = individual soul; स्वपिति *svapiti* = dreams; प्रबुद्धः *prabuddhaḥ* = awakened; पुर-त्रये *pura-traye* = in three cities; क्रीडति *krīḍati* = plays; यः *yaḥ* = who; च *ca* = and; जीवः *jīvaḥ* = individual soul; ततः *tataḥ* = from him; तु *tu* = verily; जातम् *jātam* = born; सकलम् *sakalam* = all; विचित्रम् *vicitram* = varied; आधारम् *ādhāram* = substratum; आनन्दम् *ānandam* = bliss; अखण्ड-बोधम् *akhaṇḍa-bhodham* = unbroken Consciousness; यस्मिन् *yasmin* = in whom; लयम् *layam* = dissolution; याति *yāti* = goes; पुर-त्रयम् *pura-trayam* = three cities; च *ca* = and.

14. *Again due to its connection with the deeds done in its previous births, that very same individuality* (Jıva) *comes back to the dream or the waking-state. The*

being, who sports thus in the three cities—from whom verily have sprung up all diversities, He is the substratum, the indivisible Bliss-Consciousness and in Him alone the three 'cities' go into dissolution.

"*Again*" (*Punaśca*):— After having slept and temporarily enjoyed the reviving pause from the agitations and sorrows of the waking and dream, individuality does not once for ever get extinct, but is revived again to play its part either as a waker or as a dreamer. This is our experience. But why should it emerge out? Why this painful resurrection again?

"*Through its contact with the deeds done in its previous birth*" (*Janmāntra karma yogāt*):— What makes the sleeper wake up? This has been a question that had, as in the present, so too in the past, fascinated all students of the subjective science. The final declarations of the great Masters is that it is because of the impressions and tendencies (*Vāsanā-s*) left over by thoughts entertained and actions done by the individual in his past. The truth of this statement can be demonstrated by a familiar happening in the life of every one of us.

Sleep is always disturbed when the sleeping person has an expectation of something to happen in the early hours of the following day. The expectation leaves a disturbing tendency in his mind which forces him to wake up at short intervals from his sleep. The tendencies so preserved in the mind, become active and throw up the lava of thoughts and they scorch, in their devastating flow, the cool peace of sleep. These thoughts push out into the waking-world of activities.

Similarly, the *Vāsanā-s* acquired by us in the past* will force us to come out of our restful slumber on to the fields of life to gather the harvest of our allotted experiences.

"*The very same individuality*" (*Sa eva jīvaḥ*):— The individuality in me that experiences the waking-world itself is

---

* For the exhaustion of which we have taken up this physical manifestation and have presented ourselves in our respective fields of activity.

the entity that on becoming a dreamer dreamt its dreams and it is again the same individuality that comes to live the peace of its slumber in deep sleep. In short, the "waker," the "dreamer" and the "deep-sleeper" are the three states of one and the same entity; and it is the same entity who again wakes up from sleep and becomes the "waker" to continue helplessly the life of the yesterday's "waker." The individuality remaining the same, it thus harvests on the three fields.

"The same individualised ego returns to the dream of the waking-state" (*Svapiti prabuddhaḥ*):—The happy combination of this phrase, though it renders itself to this meaning, has an enchanting suggestion all of its own. As though dreaming (*Svapiti*), wakes up (*Prabuddhaḥ*). This is reminiscent of the great *Gauḍapāda's Kārikā*. According to the author of *Māṇḍūkya Kārikā,* the Infinite Truth manifests to play under two conditions: They are :

(i) "non-apprehension of Reality" (sleep), and

(ii) "mis-apprehensions of Reality" (waking and dreaming).

Since the perceptions of the "waker" and the "dreamer," in their respective worlds of plurality are all "mis-apprehensions of reality," *Gauḍapāda* brackets them together and calls them both as dream. Here also the Seer of the *Kaivalyopaniṣad*, Lord *Brahmā* says: from the sleep, prompted and pushed out by the compelling urge of the past *Vāsanā-s*, the "deep-sleeper" arrives to reach a delusory realm of pluralistic mis-conceptions and enjoys therein his own lot in life, either as a "waker" with his conscious mind, or as a "dreamer" with his sub-conscious mind.

All these above* explanations complete the laboratory observations on life, and here follow the next stage of scientific investigation, accepted by all orthodox sciences, called analysis and deduction.

In the subjective investigation of Reality there is not much data for the seeker to work upon. The only available

---

* Ibid stanzas 11,12 and 13 first half.

field for observation is provided by one's own experiences in the three fields-of-Consciousness familiar to all of us called the waking, dream and deep-sleep. This has been advocated as an efficient path in the major *Upaniṣad-s*; for students who have developed the faculty of introspection with which they can throw themselves upon this method, it is most efficient and effective.

"The being who sports in the three cities" (*Pura-traye kriḍati yaḥ*):— The idea contained in this phrase can be illustrated from our own daily experiences. You leave your native town *Māyāvaram* and go on a holiday trip to Madras and Bangalore and return back to *Māyāvaram*. At *Māyāvaram* you are leading a comfortable and happy life with your children and you are loved and respected by all; at Madras you were honoured for one meritorious social service work you had done and at Bangalore your pocket was picked and you suffered the sorrows of starvation and the anxieties of returning home. However, you came back to your native town. Now the 'you,' an honoured personality of Madras are yourself the starving one of Bangalore, and again the same individual in you has come back to *Māyāvaram* to be respected and loved, as the father of your children.

Now, *Māyāvaram* is different from Madras, and Bangalore is different from the previous two cities; the joy of the happy family at *Māyāvaram* is a different experience from the honour you received at Madras and the dishonour you lived through in Bangalore—and yet, you can describe to your friends what happened to you in all the different cities. Because in all these diverse fields of different experiences you were the one entity that was the experiencer.

Similarly, the one common denominator, that played the parts of the "waker," the "dreamer," and the "deep sleeper" in the gross, subtle and causal bodies (*Pura-traye*), is the Self Eternal. This Consciousness Divine that illuminated the different objects and naturally therefore, had the three different sets of experiences, the One changless common factor in all of them, is the *Ātmā*, the Self. Conditioned by the gross, the subtle and the causal bodies, the Self acts as though a *Jīva* in the dream-city and in the dreamless-sleep-city.

From the standpoint of the Infinite Perfection, the Eternal Self, no doubt, this is only a recreational play, a mere sport, but by no means this is true from our standpoint. By the process of the above contemplation when we subjectively analyse ourselves, we shall develop sufficient contemplative stamina in ourselves with which we can remove ourselves from the joy and sorrow of these three familiar entities—waker, dreamer and deep-sleeper—and come to awake ourselves to the Reality behind them all.

When a dreamer awakes, his dream also rolls back into him; so too, by the above process of self-analysis and reflection when the *Jīva* wakes up to realise the God-hood, all at once the world of plurality and its finite experiences which were no doubt real to the *Jīva*, get totally annihilated and merged.

"*From Whom has sprung all diversity*" (*Tatastu Jātam Sakalam Vicitram*):—On waking up from a dream, the dreamer merges back into his waking mind and he at once realises that the entire dream, people with inert and sentient things and beings, had sprung up from his own waking-mind. In the same way, on awakening to the Divine-God Consciousness, the Self, such a Self-realised One not only does experience the end of his sense of individuality and the annihilation of the ego-projected world of plurality, but in his wisdom he also clearly visualises how *his delusory world* of joys and sorrows, consisting of matter and mind, was but a mass of *projections of his own mind on the Self*. All these have sprung up from the Absolute Consciousness alone, and the saint in the seer gets himself lost in utter wonderment, inexplicable, indescribable and unexpressible (*Vicitram*).

Very often we find the sense of wonderment* selected as an emotion to express the voiceless joy of the Divine

* Words like *Adbhūtam, Āścaryam, Vicitram* are all exclamations of wonder equivalent to "Oh!" "Ah!" "*Oośa*!" etc.

Awakening. There are some bookish *paṇḍita-s* who find fault with this technique of expression of the *Ṛṣī-s* by pointing out, very logically indeed, that this sense of wonderment is impossible in a Realised Saint because at the moment of his experience he must have transcended his mind, and has therefore, no instrument for him to feel any more emotions whatsoever. The *paṇḍita is right* in his statement but *wrong* in his understanding.

The scriptural seers have two functions to fulfil through the *Upaniṣad-s*—to declare the Truth and to reveal the same for the student. The *Upaniṣad-s* contain not only "declarations" but are also full of "revelations."

This cry of wonderment is a declaration inasmuch as it declares to me what I would be feeling when I come face to face with the vastness and splendour of the Effulgent One. It is also a *revelation* inasmuch as in my ordinary life wonder is an emotion that comes to me whenever I apprehend something that is beyond my intellect to comprehend and beyond my mind to feel. At all such experiences when my reasoning faculty is benumbed and my feelings frozen at the onslaught of an experience, I cry out "Ha! the wonder!!" The term *Vicitram*, therefore, not only declares the uniqueness of this experience of God-vision but also gives me an inkling that this revelation will reach me when I have transcended my vehicles of feeling and reasoning.

"*It is the substratum*" (*Ādhāra*):— In all ornaments gold is the *substratum*; of all waves, the ocean is the *substratum*; in all mud-pots, mud the cause, is ever present and their shapes, colours, efficiencies, names etc., are all possible only when the support of the pots, the mud exists. The *substratum is the cause* and the support; none of the above objects can exist without their *substratum (ādhāra)*. If this term is thus understood, then that which is the *Ādhāra* for the world-of-experiences* is the

* World of experiences is constituted of the perceptions of objects, the feelings of emotions and the thinking of ideas. The totality of these forms the world of our experiences in life.

Self, who is ever playing in our everyday life within ourselves as the waker, dreamer and deep-sleeper.

"*The Indivisible Bliss Consciousness*" (*Ānandam-akhaṇḍa-bodham*):— There are no vehicles in the Truth, and therefore, none of the three sorrows with which the individualised ego (*Jīva*) is persecuted can ever reach to darken the Perfect Bliss (*Ānanda*) of that condition. This is not the joy that we gain through our sense contacts with the world outside, because in all of them we know the experience is ever finite. That this "bliss" is Its nature, is now indicated by the term "unbroken" (*Akhaṇḍa*).

This Self, the Consciousness is of the nature of Knowledge, because this is the source of all our empirical knowledges. Our "awareness of things" is but a play of our Consciousness upon the objects perceived, emotions felt or ideal contemplated. Since our Consciousness is the Light that brings all our experiences into our own knowledge, it is indicated here as the "Knowledge"—*Knowledge itself*, pure and simple, and *not knowledge of anything*. It is something like "Light in itself" and not "light reflected" on any object.

"Light in itself" is not the illumination that we experience upon any object but is that which can illumine all objects that are in its medium. "*Consciousness is Knowledge itself*" when It is not playing upon any thought-wave.

"*In whom the three cities ultimately get themselves merged*" (*Yasmiṁ-llayam yāti pura-trayaṁ ca*):— The substratum for the dream-world is the waker's mind and on waking up from the dream, the very "waker" must experience that his dream has merged back into his own waking mind. Similarly, this Great Substratum-Divine of the nature of the Immutable Bliss Consciousness is not only the womb of the world of experiences but it is also the very sacred tomb of all pluralistic misconceptions.

Intellectually thus distilling away the Essential Reality

from amidst the confused medley of personalitites,[1] of identities,[2] and of their variegated experiences, the contemplator reaches the Seat of Reality, the very Self in him, and comes to experience that which is the Self alone that expresses as all these, everywhere, at all times.

एतस्माज्जायते प्राणो मनः सर्व इन्द्रियाणि च ।
खं वायुर्ज्योतिरापः पृथिवी विश्वस्य धारिणी ॥ १५ ॥

Etasmāj-jāyate prāṇo manaḥ sarva-indriyāṇi ca,
khaṁ vāyur-jyotir-āpaḥ pṛthivī viśvasya dhāriṇī.

एतस्मात् *etasmāt* = from It (Him—the Supreme Reality); जायते *jāyate* = are born; प्राण: *prāṇaḥ* = *prāṇa*, vital air (life); मन: *manaḥ* = mind (*antaḥkaraṇa*); सर्व इन्द्रियाणि *sarva-indriyāṇi* = all organs; च *ca* = and; खम् *kham* = the space (sky, *ākāśa*); वायु: *vāyuḥ* = air (the wind); ज्योति: *jyotiḥ* = the fire; आप: *āpaḥ* = the water; पृथिवी *pṛthivī* = the earth; विश्वस्य *viśvasya* = all (the universe); धारिणी *dhāriṇī* = supporter.

15. *From Him are born* the Prāṇa *(life), the mind (*Antaḥkaraṇa*), all the organs, the sky (*Ākāśa*), the wind (*Vāyu*), the fire (*Jyotiḥ*), the water (*Āpaḥ*) and the earth (*Pṛthivī*) which supports all.*

This is a *Mantra* that also occurs in the *Muṇḍakopaniṣad* (II-i-3). "The substratum (*Ādhāra*) for all effects is but the very material cause from which they have sprung up" is a well-known fact. This is the *Ātman*, the Self, which has been described in the three previous stanzas as the very material cause for "the manifestation of all activities in the body" (*Prāṇa*), for the mind (*Antaḥkaraṇa*) that correlates all perceptions and responses, and for all the sense organs of both perceptions and action. The intellect, mind and the sense-organs in an individual (*Prāṇī*) in whom life (*Prāṇa*) is fully manifest can function only in a field

1. Physical, mental and intellectual entities.
2. As waker, dreamer and deep-sleeper.

of potential experiences. The sense-organs, mind and intellect when alive are capable of perceiving, feeling and thinking, but they can do so only in a field of objects, feeling and thoughts. A car, where there are no roads, a boat in a stretch of sandy desert, music for the deaf, a printed scripture for the blind, are all useless because there are no fields for these vehicles to functions.

Thus a conducive field[1] that can yield endless experiences is unavoidable if the living body-mind-intellect, sprung from the Ultimate Truth, the *Ādhāra*, must function and gain their experiences. This field-of-objects is constituted of the great Five Elements, sprung from the same Eternal Divine Self. The grossified[2] five Elements, their mutual admixture, the entire gross world-of-objects, and those Five Great Elements in their rudimentary state (*Tanmātrā-s*) constitute the material from which feelings and thoughts are moulded out.

यत्परं ब्रह्म सर्वात्मा विश्वस्यायतनं महत् ।
सूक्ष्मात्सूक्ष्मतरं नित्यं तत्त्वमेव त्वमेव तत् ॥ १६ ॥

yatparaṁ brahma sarvātmā viśvasyā-yatanaṁ mahat,
sūkṣmāt-sūkṣmataraṁ nityaṁ tat-tvameva tvameva tat.

यत् *yat* = which; परम् *param* = supreme; ब्रह्म *brahma* = *Brahman*; सर्व-आत्मा *sarva-ātmā* = the Self in all; विश्वस्य *viśvasya* = of the Universe; आयतनम् *āyatanam* = support; महत् *mahat* = great; सूक्ष्मात् *sūkṣmāt* = than Subtle; सूक्ष्मतरम् *sūkṣmataram* = subtler; नित्यम् *nityam* = eternal; तत् *tat* = that; त्वम् *tvam* = thou; एव *eva* = alone; त्वम् *tvam* = thou; एव *eva* = alone; तत् *tat* = that

16. *That which is the Supreme* Brahman, *the Self in all, the ample Support of the Universe, Subtler than the subtle and Eternal... That alone thou art, thou alone art that.*

---

1. Both the gross outer world and the subtler inner world.
2. *Pañcikṛtam* : Elements that have gone through the process of the five-fold self-division and mutual recombination—Refer *Ātmabodha* Stanza 12.

Intellect can understand only the objective world and the student, erudite and intelligent, had reached the feet of the teacher with a highly sharpened and clear intellect. The teacher has to address the student's intellect and so he must give the student a method of intellectual investigation whereby he can himself apprehend the Truth. But in the process, there is a great unavoidable contadiction. Though we apply the intellectual processes in explaining and demonstrating the play of the Spirit in and through matter, the student has not only to appreciate intellectually the declarations of the teacher but he must ultimately come to experience the great subjective Reality in himself.

Due to the very nature of the discussions and the methods employed for detecting the play of the Self in the various States of Consciousness, the intellectual faculty in the student would, in its understanding, come to recognise the great Eternal *Brahman* as "*That*" from which the instruments-of-experiences and the fields-of-objects have arisen. The student would naturally understand the reality as "*That,*" meaning as something other than himself—far away in time and place, where he might reach at some future date, as a result of, perhaps, an inexplicable miracle!

Such a conclusion is not unintelligent but spiritually it is extremely wrong— a foolish mistake. To avoid such a mis-understanding in the student, the teacher explains in the stanza under discussion, that this Divine Eternal *Brahman* is nothing but the very spiritual essence in the seeker.

"*The soul of all*" (*Sarvātmā*):—That which is the Supreme Self is all-pervading and is the very Essence in all names and forms—of all that we perceive in the outer world of every thought and feeling that we experience within. Just as the ocean is the "soul" in all the waves, *Brahman* is the Essential Presence in everything everywhere.

"*The ample support of the Universe*" (*Viśvasya-Āyatanam-Mahat*):— In philosophy when they use the term "support" or substratum (*Āyatanam*) it means something more than what meets our ears. It is not used here in the sense we say, "the book is supported by your table." In this case, the book is something other than the table. Also, the book and you can at any time exchange the supports and then the table becomes your support and the chair, the support for the book. Lastly, instead of you sitting alone on the chair, if the whole family of yours were to sit on the same chair, the poor chair can get crushed under the load. In Philosophy, to understand thus would lead us to an absurd conclusion that the Reality is now being crushed by the very load of the pluralistic world.

Ocean is the "support" of the waves; gold is the support of the ornaments; the cotton is the suport of the textiles. It is in this sense the word "support" (*Āyatanam*) is used in philosophy. *Brahman* is the very material cause of the Universe. Just as mud, the material cause of the cup, ever "supports" the cup, the Universe of plurality also is ever "supported" by the Infinite *Brahman*.

The adjective "ample" (*Mahat*) qualifying "support" is used only perhaps to indicate that the entire Universe (*Viśva*) is only a disturbance in an insignificant part* of the Infinite.

"*Subtler than the subtle*" (*Sūkṣmāt-sūkṣmataram*):— Describing the *Brahman*, which is the very essence of the universe, this familiar scriptural idiom is used. In philosophy subtlety is measured by its pervasiveness. That which pervades more is subtler; that which is the subtlest is the most pervading and therefore, that which is "subtler than subtlest" must necessarily be all-pervading. *Brahman* pervades all. *Brahman* is not only the soul or the core in all names and forms (*Sarva ātmā*) but is also the source of all. It pervades everything and nothing pervades it. Everything is *Brahman* Itself. When we say, the "dream-world" is supported by the waker's mind, we

---

* *"Viṣṭabhya aham idaṁ kṛtsanam eka amiśena sthito jagat"—Bh. Gītā* X-42.
"Atyatiṣṭhad-daśāṅgulam"—Puruṣa Sūktam-1.

mean that everything in the dream is nothing but in essence that waker's own mind.

"*Eternal*" (*Nityam*):—That which is the All-pervading is Unconditioned by anything and therefore, finitude which is the destiny of all the conditioned things, can never contaminate the Infinite. Though the substratum for the world of names and forms is *Brahman*, the All-pervading is ever changeless and Eternal.

Even after this much of discussion the student will comprehend the Truth only as an object or a "factor" that has got all these qualities. To end this misconception and to divert his attention unto himself, the *Upaniṣad Ṛṣī-s* thunder forth the staggering conmmandment: "That Thou Art."

"*That alone thou art*" (*Tat tvam eva*):—"That" here means "that which you have just now understood intellectually as an object of your knowledge." That is not anything other than you, but is the very essence of yourself.

"*That*" may be me...."*That*" being Divine, "*That*" can play in me... but, also, I am *myself* and I know "*That*"—this would be the inner silent cry of the spiritual desparado even in the best of the students. The ocean may be the cause for the waves, but the wave in its limited dimension, shape, form, power and strength fails to comprehend that it can ever be the ocean.

To blast out this intellectual sense of distinction the teacher in the same breath adds, "Thou alone art that" (*Tvam eva tat*). When an individual thus, through a total and diligent observations and analysis of himself playing as the waker, the dreamer and the deep-sleeper, comes to detect his own identity with the "common factor" in all the three, in this subjective moments of deep meditation, he shall come to experience that the Self in him is the Self everywhere, the *Brahman*.

This sacred declaration "*Tat tvam-eva tvam-eva tat*" is the commandment (*Upadeśa vākya*) of the Seer of the *Upaniṣad* to his students. To realise it subjectively in the individual bosom by the student himself, for himself, is the path of the highest realisation called meditation. How this meditation is conducted is the theme of the following few stanzas.

जाग्रत्स्वप्नसुषुप्त्यादिप्रपञ्चं यत्प्रकाशते ।
तद्ब्रह्माहमिति ज्ञात्वा सर्वबन्धैः प्रमुच्यते ॥ १७ ॥

Jāgrat-svapna-suṣuptyādi—
prapañcaṁ yat-prakāśate,
tad-brahmāham-iti jñātvā
sarva-bandhaiḥ pramucyate.

जाग्रत्-स्वप्न-सुषुप्त्यादि-प्रपञ्चम् *jāgrat-svapna-suṣupti-ādi prapañcam* = the worlds of waking, dream and deep-sleep etc.; यत् *yat* = which; प्रकाशते *prakāśate* = illumines; तत् *tat* = that; ब्रह्म *brahma* = *Brahman*; अहम् *aham* = I; इति *iti* = thus; ज्ञात्वा *jñātvā* = realising, by knowing; सर्व-बन्धैः *sarva-bandhaiḥ* = from all shackles; प्रमुच्यते *pramucyate* = is released or liberated.

17. *"That which illumines the world of relative experiences lived in the waking, dream and deep-sleep conditions, that* Brahman *am I"—and realising thus, one is liberated from all shackles.*

In the light of what we have discussed so far, the very translation is self-explanatory. The One Consciousness is aware of all happenings in all the three states. The Principle of Knowledge that illumines all experiences in the waking, dreaming and deep-sleep conditions is one and the same. It is this Self, playing among the objects, that acquires to itself the false sense of individuality as the waker, dreamer and deep-sleeper. Devoid of all trappings, the Pure Consciousness, undressed from all its matter vestures, is the consistent Reality that ever plays behind the concept of our delusory ego-sense. To rediscover this identity with the Self is to experience "That *Brahman* am I" (*Tat Brahma aham*).

This is to be brought into our experience; and it is not sufficient if we note it or appreciate it. We must be able to recognise, re-visualise, re-live that we are not the limited ego but are in fact this *Brahman*. On thus awakening to the experience of Self, the man of God-consciousness "*gets released from all shackles*."

Personality shackles are not physical chains on the limbs of the anatomy, but they are more painful and self-destructive. The limitations created in the expression of our individuality—due to the endless hungers of the body, the innumerable agitations of the mind and the painful restlessness of the intellect—are what we call in philosophy as the "bondages" (*Bandhaiḥ*).

If we carefully diagnose the disease, we shall find that the outer-world of objects and beings are helpless to make or unmake us. But it is our own unintelligent relationship with the world around us that creates the shackles. When once the true nature of the Self-Divine is understood, naturally it becomes easy for the individual to maintain and assert his right to relationship with the world outside and to come out of all the sense of bondages in himself.

The stanza, as it stands, give us an inkling as to what should be a meditator's attitude towards himself. When he is arriving at and continuing to be in the Still Centre in himself, the seeker will find it hard to reach a still moment of peaceful contemplation, because the mind will bring into him streams of its volcanic contents and the flowing lava of desires, which can scorch the peace in the field of meditation. Once it gets active in the noisy fire-works of its explosions, serene silence is shattered by the clamouring tongues of a thousand sense-cravings. At such a moment what the poor meditator should do? The advice to him is implied in the following *Mantra*.

त्रिषु धामसु यद्भोग्यं भोक्ता भोगश्च यद्भवेत् ।
तेभ्यो विलक्षणः साक्षी चिन्मात्रोऽहं सदाशिवः ॥ १८ ॥

Triṣu dhāmasu yad-bhogyaṁ
bhoktā bhogaś-ca yad-bhavet,
tebhyo vilakṣaṇaḥ sākṣī
cin-mātro-'haṁ sadāśivaḥ.

त्रिषु *triṣu* = in the three; धामसु *dhāmasu* = realms; यत् *yat* = which; भोग्यम् *bhogyam* = enjoyable; भोक्ता *bhoktā* = enjoyer; भोग: *bhogaḥ* = enjoyment; च *ca* = and; यत् *yat* = which; भवेत् *bhavet* = can be; तेभ्य: *tebhyaḥ* = from them; विलक्षण: *vilakṣaṇaḥ* = different; साक्षी *sākṣī* = witness; चिन्मात्र: *cinmātraḥ* = Pure Consciousness; अहम् *aham* = I; सदाशिव: *sadāśivaḥ* = Ever Auspicious.

18. *All that constitutes the enjoyable, the enjoyer and the enjoyment in the three realms... different from them all am I, the Witness, the Ever-auspicious, Pure Consciousness.*

Relative experiences can take place only when the object of experience is contacted by the experiencer through the instruments of experiences, the sense organs. No experience is ever possible without the three fundamental factors that constitute an experience called :

(a) the experiencer (*Bhoktā*),

(b) the experienced (*Bhogyam*), and

(c) the favourable relationship between the above two, called the experiencing (*Bhoga*).

The subject, the object and the relationship between them are technically considered as the three factors without which no experience can ever take place— be it during our waking, dream or deep-sleep. "Different *(Vilakṣaṇaḥ)* from them all is '*me*' the Self"— is the understanding that we gather from the previous *mantrā-s* of this scripture.

By this process we totally deny and negate all empirical experiences of the pluralistic phenomenal world. "Negation of the false" is the first stage in the *Yoga* of Meditation. The second stage which is that of "*the assertion of the True*" is indicated here by the declaration "*the Witness, the Ever-auspicious, Pure Consciousness am I.*"

By asserting that the Pure Consciousness is neither the waker, waking and the objects perceived, nor the dreamer, the dreaming, and the dream-objects, nor the sleeper, the sleeping and the total absence of everything in the deep-sleep; the teacher is pointing out a transcendental experience which is unlike all our present experiences.

In order to reach this realm of God-consciousness, we are not to involve ourselves in them but must learn to transcend and steadily come away entirely from their clutches. The art, of thus keeping ourselves away from them, is to stand by and observe them as a witness (*Sākṣī*). Just as, the sun is a witness of all that is happening in the world and yet is not involved in them—although none of the activities of the world would be possible without the sun—the *Ātman*, the Self, is a mere Witness of all that is happening in Its light and around It. To identity ourselves with this Self is to train ourselves to be a witness of all our physical perceptions, mental feelings and intellectual thoughts.

A witness is one who, with no personal interest, is steadily watching what is happening in front of him. From the balcony of my house I can be a witness of a procession only so long as the procession is going along my street. When the tail end of the procession also has crawled out of my street around the corner, I, who was a witness till then, is now myself alone, complete in myself.

Similarly, this "attitude of a witness" (*Sākṣī bhāva*) to all that is happening at the different layers of my personality is possible for me only so long as things are happening in them. When once I stand apart from the happenings, merely watching, in disinterested detachment, the mad revelry of matter slowly ebbs away, because these are essentially inert matter and can giggle out to parade in dynamic expressions only with my support. When I sit back, idly observing, unpatronised by me, the procession slowly dies away and what remains would be "the witness minus the field of objects witnessed."

Conscious of the objects I become a witness. When the objects fade away, no more a witness am I. The witness in me thus becomes "the faculty that gave me the capacity to witness" what all were happening in front of me. This Pure Consciousness with no objects (*Cinmātra*) is the Supreme Self, Unconditioned and Free, Immaculate and Perfect which is the Reality behind the universe.

This "Objectless awareness" (*Cinmātra*) is unconditioned and unlimited and therefore, all the causes for disturbance and distractions have ended in it and thus it is Ever-auspicious (*Sadā-śiva*).

The previous stanza gives us an indication that "I am the *Brahman* which illumines all experiences," which as we said earlier is meditation. But in order to reach this field of meditation, the path is to withdraw our grace from our own vehicles, which is to be achieved by remaining "in the attitude of a witness" in ourselves. When as a result of this process, the storm of the mind has calmed down and even the last of their ripples has gone ashore, the pure waters of Truth shall reflect the brilliant glories of the *Cidākāśa*: "*I am that Pure Consciousness alone, Ever-auspicious*."

मय्येव सकलं जातं मयि सर्वं प्रतिष्ठितम् ।
मयि सर्वं लयं याति तद्ब्रह्माद्वयमस्म्यहम् ॥ १९ ॥

Mayyeva sakalaṁ jātaṁ mayi sarvaṁ pratiṣṭhitam,
mayi sarvaṁ layaṁ yāti tadbrahmā-dvayam-asmyaham.

मयि *mayi* = in me; एव *eva* = alone; सकलम् *sakalam* = everything, all; जातम् *jātam* = is born; मयि *mayi* = in me; सर्वम् *sarvam* = all; प्रतिष्ठितम् *pratiṣṭhitam* = established; मयि *mayi* = in me; सर्वम् *sarvam* = all; लयम् *layam* = is dissolved; याति *yāti* = gets, goes; तद्

tad = That; ब्रह्म *brahma* = *Brahman*; अद्वयम् *advayam* = non-dual; अस्मि *asmi* = am; अहम् *aham* = I.

19. *In me alone everything is born; in me alone does everything exist and in me alone gets everything dissolved. I am That non-dual* Brahman.

The effects can never remain away from their cause; they are all born from their cause; they exist in their cause, and even if the manifested effects were to end their particular expressions, they can merge back only to become one with their cause. The waves arise from, exist in and merge back into the ocean. The ornaments arise from, exist in and merge back to become gold. Similarly, the entire phenomenal pluralities that provide our world of relative experiences, arise from *Brahman*, the Supreme Consciousness, exist in It and when the Higher is experienced, the lower merges back into It alone. *Brahman* is the world's substratum ultimately (*That non-dual Brahman am I*).

When we pass from one plane-of-consciousness into another, we cannot ever smuggle into the new plane, anything from the earlier one. Perfect iron curtains exist between the waking, dream and deep-sleep states. At the frontiers, the high tariff-walls built in massive strength are most efficiently guarded. The waking world's successes, joys or relations cannot cross over its frontiers into the dreaming state. The dreamer's realm cannot peep over the frontiers that mark out the dark domain of the deep-sleep. To the waker alone is the waking world to enjoy. The dreamer alone can rule over the dream-kingdom. The sleeper has no admission either to the phantasies of the dreamland or to the wonders of the waking world.

From this it is evidently clear that when the ego ends in the spiritual awakening, when the experience of the Pure *Brahman* is opened up, as *Brahman* one must experience therein the total merger of the entire world experienced by the ego earlier. Just as the waker can cry out that his earlier dream has merged back into himself, and can also recognise that everything he saw in the dream was only a projection of his own waking mind; so too, through meditation when the student transcends everything and ends himself up in the *experience of the Absolute*, the "*roar of realisation*" that will thunder through his silent heart *is the content of this mantra.*

In the none too perceptible logic of thought that connects the four *mantrā-s* (15-18) lies concealed a sacred truth which is the highest secret in the technique of meditation. First the commandment of *Ṛṣī-s*[1] (*Upadeśa*) which is to be logically analysed intellectually disccused and clearly understood[2]; thereafter (in *mantra*-16) is described the subjective reflection (*Manana*) of the Truth declaration (*Upadeśa*). Here is an attempt to realise *that One Factor which is the sport of* the Waker, the Dreamer and the Deep-Sleeper. The world around us being what it is, the difficulty experienced by the students is not so much in their inability to consistently contemplate upon this constant Consciousness, but it is in the fact that contemplation gets dissipated by the disturbances that reach the mind through the sense organs. Thereafter, the intellect dances away easily into them to be lost in the triple sport of the enjoyer, enjoyed and enjoying. To control the mind's impulses, without ourselves getting involved in them, is the technique which is explained[3] as the *witness attitude*.

By this process when the thoughts of the mind come themselves to rest in peace, the pluralistic world of three states of Consciousness (*prapañca*) ebbs away leaving the individual on the great rock of Truth, from which all are born, in which everything exists and into which alone all merge back. This *mantra* under discussion, is the *roar of Divine experience*. A few of the following *mantrā-s* give the various indicative definitions of this unique and voiceless experience of the spiritual Truth, the *Brahman*.

1. *Tad tvameva tvameva tat.*—Ibid *Mantra*-16
2. *Tat-buddhayaḥ*—Refer discourse on *Gītā* V-17.
3. Ibid *Mantra*-18

अणोरणीयानहमेव तद्वन्
महानहं विश्वमहं विचित्रम् ।
पुरातनोऽहं पुरुषोऽहमीशो
हिरण्मयोऽहं शिवरूपमस्मि ॥ २० ॥

Aṇor-aṇīyān-aham-eva tadvan
mahān-ahaṁ viśvam-ahaṁ vicitram,
purātano-'haṁ puruṣo-'ham-īśo
hiraṇyamayo-'haṁ śiva-rūpam-asmi.

अणो: *aṇoḥ* = than atom, smallest particle; अणीयान् *aṇīyān* = smaller; अहम् *aham* = I; एव *eva* = alone; तद्वत् *tadvat* = similarly; महान् *mahān* = great; अहम् *aham* = I; विश्वम् *viśvam* = universe; अहम् *aham* = I; विचित्रम् *vicitram* = varied; पुरातन: *purātanaḥ* = ancient; अहम् *aham* = I; पुरुष: *puruṣaḥ* = *Puruṣa*, the Soul; अहम् *aham* = I; ईश: *īśaḥ* = Ruler; हिरण्यमय: *hiraṇyamayaḥ* = Effulgent; अहम् *aham* = I; शिव-रूपम् *śiva-rūpam* = form of auspiciousness; अस्मि *asmi* = am.

20. *I am smaller than the smallest and also am I the most vast. I am the manifold universe—amazing; I am the Ancient One, the* Puruṣa; *the Supreme Ruler am I, the Effulgent One, by nature ever-auspicious.*

In the Absolute, dimensions are impossible. In the relative world, without the concept of dimensions, no gross experience is ever possible. Therefore, to explain to us the dimension-less Infinitude, the teachers will have to use the ordinary language employing a novel technique of expression. The Unknown is to be indicated, because Truth, as such, is unknown to us now. The unknown can be indicated only by the terms of the known. The definition of the Unknown given out in terms of the known explains the language delicacy in all scriptures of the world.

This is something like the usual problems given in elementary geometry wherein you are to discover the unknown point 'C' when two known points 'A' and 'B' are known. The unknown 'C' is defined in terms of the known 'A' and 'B.' It is defined then that 'C' is that point which is a given number of inches from 'A' and a definite known distance from 'B.' Though 'C' when once it is discovered has no relationship either with 'A' or with 'B,' yet to facilitate our discovery of 'C' we can make use of 'A' and 'B' as a pleasant convenience. Similarly, the concepts of time, place, distance etc., which really belong to the realm of the finite, are made use of to fix up the unknown point of our enquiry and seeking in ourselves. And as the point "C" in geometry, when once discovered becomes an entity in itself, totally independent of 'A' and 'B,' so too when this Great Truth is realised everything else is transcended.

"Smaller than the Smallest and also the Most Vast":— The moment we are told that the Truth is smaller than the smallest, the intellect can comprehend It; when the *mantra* declares that it is vaster than the vast, the intellect can understand It. Concepts of vast-ness and minute-ness are easily appreciated by the intellect. But in the world outside these two contrary qualities can never remain as qualities of one and the same object. Thus through the known meaning, that which is comprehensible, the All-pervading Reality is indicated. The all-pervading space is there in the minutest channel in the hair, at once being the space in which the universe moves about, explore themselves out and reform themselves again. The stanza in its opening line reminds us of other scriptures where we have similar expressions.[1]

"I am the manifold Universe ...... amazing!" (*Vicitram*):— In the stillness of meditation when the All-pervasiveness is apprehended, the pluralistic worlds, perceived, felt and thought dissolve themselves to be the Non-dual Reality and I, the Spirit alone, thereafter, exists. This experience is the end of all personalities and the individual ego stands dumb-founded, still stultified in the staggering revelation. This is indicated by the

---

1. (i) *"Dūrāt sudūre tad-ihāntike ca—Muṇḍaka* (III-i-7)
(ii) ....*Tad dure tadvantike,*
tad-antarasya sarvasya tadu sarvasyāsya bāhyataḥ (*Īśa Up. Verse*-5);
(iii) Aṇoraṇīyān-mahato mahīyān.......Kaṭha Up. (I-ii-20): etc.

term "amazing." We have already explained the significance of the term *Vicitram* in an earlier *mantra*.

"*I am the Ancient One*":—Truth is ever *Sanātana* and never modern—newly found out or recently invented. Everything discovered has an existence even before the date of its discovery, although it was then lying hidden behind a veil of non-apprehension. This ignorance is lifted up with the knowledge and the apprehended Truth is recognised and experienced as that which was always present.

Today we apprehend only the experience of the conditioned Consciousness. Every moment of our experience we are *conscious of* all our experiences viz. objects, feelings and thoughts. This continuous process of 'Knowing' is the very substance of the limited individuality, in the dream, be it in the waking or in the profound sleep in our life. When from the sense of individuality all the objects as well as the instruments of experience are eliminated, the 'objectless Consciousness' is experienced as such. This experience cannot be anything totally new because we always know by it—all our knowing at all times was only a play of this Principle of Knowledge. Thus the Truth that we discover through meditation is not anything new. It is the Ancient One.

"*Puruṣa*":—The Conscious Spirit that vitalises all the inert matter layers around us (*Prakṛti*), both in their gross and subtle form is called the *Puruṣa*. The presiding deity in whose light and glory the inert matter springs up into dynamic existence, vibrant with its abilites, capacities and capabilities, physical, mental and intellectual is called the *Puruṣa*; "I am the *Puruṣa*, the Ancient One."

"*The Ruler*" (*Īśa*):—In *Saṁskṛta Īśa* means the Controller, the Governor, the Regulator, the one who gives all powers of expression to all organs and limbs.

The proprietor of a firm, in that firm; the father of a family, in his own family; the autocratic King, in his own kingdom, are all examples of their lordship in their own fields. Nothing happens in a field that is not sanctioned by its overlord and everything that is happening in his domain is ordered, regulated, controlled and administered by the Master of the domain. The life presiding over the various personalities in us is the one factor without whom none of the expressions of the life is possible in us. And it is He who, with His mere presence lends His power for the vehicles to express according to their own cultivated tendencies.*

"*I am the Effulgent One*" (*Hiraṇamaya aham*) and the term "*I am Ever-auspicious*" (*Śivarūpam asmi*):—have been both already discussed in the earlier *mantrā-s*. Pure Consciousness is a subjective light in which all our experiences are brought home to our knowledge. In this sense of the term, Consciousness can be considered as the "Light" that illumines every knowledge.

Where there are no conditioning vehicles of experience, there cannot be even a trace of sorrow, since sorrow is but mental agitation. The greater the agitation, the greater the sorrow, and conversely, lesser the agitation, lesser the sorrow. At the moment of awakening into the Pure, Spiritual Consciousness, mind has totally been transcended and where the mind has ended, all inauspiciousness must also have ended. The Truth is thus indicated by the term "All auspiciousness" (*Śiva rūpam*).

It must be closely observed that in this stanza the familiar terms of the *Upaniṣad-s* are used as indicative definitions of the Eternal Reality. It is not a discussion, it is an open declaration of the Seer's subjective experience: '*I am*' (*Asmi*).

अपाणिपादोऽहमचिन्त्यशक्तिः
पश्याम्यचक्षुः स श्रृणोम्यकर्णः ।
अहं विजानामि विविक्तरूपो
न चास्ति वेत्ता मम चित्सदाऽहम् ॥ २१ ॥

* For futher reading on this concept refer Discourses on *Bh. Gītā* (V-14).

Apāṇipādo-'ham-acintya-śaktiḥ
paśyāmy-acakṣuḥ sa śṛṇomy-akarṇaḥ,
ahaṁ vijānāmi vivikta-rūpo
na cāsti vettā mama cit-sadā-'ham.

अपाणि-पाद: *apāṇi-pādaḥ* = without hands and legs; अहम् *aham* = I; अचिन्त्य-शक्ति: *acintya-śaktiḥ* = incomprehensible power; पश्यामि *paśyāmi* = see; अचक्षु: *acakṣuḥ* = without eyes; स: *saḥ* = that; शृणोमि *śṛṇomi* = (I) hear; अकर्ण: *akarṇaḥ* = without ears; अहम् *aham* = I; विजानामि *vijānāmi* = know; विविक्त-रूप: *vivikta-rūpaḥ* = devoid of form; न *na* = not; च *ca* = and; अस्ति *asti* = is; वेत्ता *vettā* = knower; मम *mama* = my; चित् *cit* = pure knowledge; सदा *sadā* = always; अहम् *aham* = I.

21. I am without hands and legs, of incomprehensible power. I see without eyes, hear without ears. Devoid of all forms, I am knowing (everything) and there is none that knows me. I am ever Pure-Knowledge.

Continuing the "*roar of fulfilment*" the man of realisation in the Seer outshines himself in each wave of his poetic inspiration as the *mantrā-s* tumble out of his heart of beatitude. The words here can remind us of similar phrases used in *Bṛhadāraṇyaka Upaniṣad.*

"*I am without hands and legs*" (*Apāṇi-pādo-aham*):—In such a special use of language, wherein words are used as technical expressions, they should not be understood in their direct word-meanings. If we accept here the word-meaning, the *Hindū* concept of God needs immediate protection and patronage from some "Society for the Disabled!" Here, the hands and legs are representatives of the five instruments of action with which all of us express our responses to the world outside, no doubt in each one, the mode of response is ordered by his own powerful *Vāsanā-s*. When we say that the Truth has no hands and legs, it only means that "Truth is the power that functions in the hands and legs but Itself has no hands and legs."[1] This is as logical as if one were to say "electricity has no bulbs" or that the "petrol has no engine." In short, it only indicates for the contemplative intellect of the student that the Pure Consciousness in us has no need to respond to the world-of-objects outside and that It is the life giving touch that functions in all living hands and legs.

"Incomprehensible Power" (*Acintya Śaktiḥ*):— Regarding Life in all Its purity,[2] all that we can say is that It is a power that cannot be comprehended. In fact all energies, even in the physical gross world, are recognised only when they manifest as perceptible expressions. The Infinite Life, One without a second, that functions as the soul of every name and form in the universe can only be understood as a Great Power, experienceable only on transcending the intellect, which cannot think of It, because It is the very Power in the intellect which expresses as intelligence in the intellect.

"I see without eyes" (*Paśyāmi Acakṣuḥ*), *"I hear without ears"* (*Śṛṇomi Akarṇaḥ*):— This is a famous statement known the world over. In its directness, delicacy of finish and neat beauty, this decalaration has captivated all great minds. It says that the seer in the eyes is the Truth which through the eyes illumines the objects in front of the eyes. Similarly, the Self is the hearer in the ears. The entire *Kenopaniṣad* uses up the full length of its canvas in painting this idea in all its details and colourful imports. The instruments of experiences (i.e. body, mind and intellect) and the objects of experiences (i.e. perceived objects, experienced emotions and known thoughts) are both not the *Ātman* and the Self is that which is beyond the instruments, the Eternal Subject which through the instuments is aware of all the objects. It is the "hearing power" behind the ears in a field of sound—the seeking intelligence behind the eyes in a field of forms and colours.

1. *Sarvataḥ-pāṇi-pādaṁ tat sarvato-'kṣi-śirōmukham—Bh. Gītā* XIII-13
2. Devoid of all Its conditionings and therefore away from all impressions.

"Devoid of forms" (*Vivikta rūpaḥ*):—That which is unconditioned by the instruments-of-action and by the instruments-of-perception, as indicated above, must be something that has no form, since our forms are provided by our physical bodies. In saying so, the student may misunderstand the *Ātman* to be the "subtle body" constituted of the instruments of knowing, experienced by us as feeling or thinking. To deny this probable fallacy that It is the mind and intellect, the *mantra* declares that the Self is the Knowledge.

"I know" (*Aham Vijānāmi*):—Our entire intellectual life is a constant procession of endless assertions of "I know." Therefore, here again the reflective student reflecting upon the immediate suggestion of this term might come to the false understanding that the intellect that knows everything may be the Truth, the Ultimate Reality. To eliminate this confusion it is said :

"There is none that knows Me" (*Na ca asti vettā mama*):—Even the ideas in the intellect are illuminated by the Consciousness. We are conscious of all thoughts that arise in our mind and intellect—good and bad, knowledge and ignorance, memory and forgetfulness, the endless variety of emotions and types of feelings........ whatever that arises at the intellect-mind level is illumined by Consciousness. To indicate this Consciousness as the Absolute Subject is the burden of the teacher's song here. All that the teacher has said so far, has no doubt dragged us from the outer realm of the sense organs into the innermost sanctum of the intellect.

But even the intellectual ideas belong to the world of objects illumined by the Consciousness and therefore, the teacher says there is *none that knows me*; I am the ultimate subject in myself. As related to me, everything in me and in the outer world is an object for me to know. There is no knowledge that can know me as an object of its knowledge. This final summing up is given in the last phrase in the *mantra*.

"*I am ever the Pure Knowledge*" (*Cit-sadā-aham*):— I am Knowledge Pure without any object for It to illumine other than Itself. This Non-dual Knowledge which is All-pervading with its own Effulgence has no field or plurality to illumine. "This Immutable-Knowledge-Absolute am I always" (*Sadā*), is the confident roar of the final spiritual experience.

On waking up from the dream, inspite of the dream experiences, I instantaneously recognise that I have ever been in my own bed and had never made any pilgrimage to any distant lands, and that the strange situations and experiences were the hallucinations of the Consciousness 'Absolute' (*Cit-sadā-aham*), the experience is that I had never been ever really in the trap of death, which was but a hallucination thrown up by a mind in its brutal mischief.

In this *mantra* there is a pun upon the term "*Vivikta-rūpa*" meaning "devoid of all forms." If there be anything that is devoid of all forms, then our sense organs cannot perceive it and therefore, it is different from all. In the context of this stanza when the *Ṛṣi* makes this statement after indicating that the Truth is something other than the organs of action and perception, this can only mean a total negation of the mind and intellect. In this sense, then the Truth is pointedly indicated by the statement that "I am the knowing Principle" which has no other knower to know 'It' —"I am Pure Knowledge."

If *Kaivalyopaniṣad* is a rare piece of jewellery in the vaults of the *Hindū* culture, we can without any hesitation, declare that this stanza is the precious pendant of beauty that enriches this piece of jewellery.

वेदैरनेकैरहमेव वेद्यो
वेदान्तकृद्वेदविदेव चाहम् ।
न पुण्यपापे मम नास्ति नाशो
न जन्म देहेन्द्रिय बुद्धिरस्ति ॥ २२ ॥

Vedair-anekair-aham-eva vedyo
vedānta-kṛd-veda-vid-eva cāham,
na puṇya-pāpe mama nāsti nāśo
na janma dehendriya buddhir-asti.

वेदैः *vedaiḥ* = by *Vedā-s*; अनेकैः *anekaiḥ* = different; अहम् *aham* = I; एव *eva* = alone; वेद्यः *vedyaḥ* = to be known; वेदान्त-कृद् *vedānta-kṛd* = revealer of the *Upaniṣad-s*; वेद-विद् *veda-vid* = knower of the *Veda*; एव *eva* = alone; च *ca* = and; अहम् *aham* = I; न *na* = not; पुण्य-पापे *puṇya-pāpe* = merit and demerit; मम *mama* = my; न *na* = not; अस्ति *asti* = is; नाशः *nāśaḥ* = destruction; न *na* = not; जन्म-देह-इन्द्रिय बुद्धिः *janma-deha-indriya buddhiḥ* = idea of birth, body and senses; अस्ति *asti* = is.

22. *I alone am the theme taught in the different* Vedā-s, *I am the revealer of the* Upaniṣad-s, *the* Vedānta *and I alone am the real knower of the* Vedā-s. *For me there is neither merit nor demerit. I suffer no destruction. I have neither birth nor body, nor sense organs, nor the mind-intellect equipment.*

To say that this stanza is reminiscent of the *Gītā* would be implying that chronologically this *Upaniṣad* must have been written on a much later date than the *Gītā*; if the same statement is reversed to express that the *Gītā* has borrowed the very same phraseology of this *mantra,** it would make the *Upaniṣad* older than the *Gītā*. No doubt, a lot of research has been done, started by the Western scholars and efficiently taken up by our Professors. But it is very difficult to fix these with any authoritative finality. In our utter reverence to the culture and the cultural textbooks of Divine origin, it is safer that we only note that there is a happy similarity in the ideas and expressions in the *Upaniṣad-s* and the *Gītā*. A seeker's spiritual development is in no way lesser by not ascertaining which text is earlier and which is later, in chronology. Let professional inspectors of books exhaust themselves in this futile controversy.

* Refer to *Bh. Gītā* ... the second half of XV-15.

"The theme in the various Vedā-s (Vedaiḥ anekaiḥ aham eva vedyaḥ):—The *Vedā-s*, be it in its *mantra* portion or the *Brāhmaṇa* section or the *Upaniṣadik* chapter, all of them are invoking, approaching and realising the one and the same Infinite Reality, the One golden chord of Uniformity that holds all together. Throughout the *Vedik* textbooks, this is the core and their theme, the burden of their songs. The *Mantrā-s* adore the Mighty Omnipotent Power of Infinite beauty that expresses Itself through the phenomena around; the entire cosmos is an insignificant expression of the Supreme Self, the *Paramātmā*. The *Brāhmaṇa* portion through its elaborate ritualism helps the seekers to approach the experience of this Reality. The *Upaniṣad* section describes the approach to this Truth, the nature of the Truth and the final subtle methods of realising the Truth, through the delicate methods of contemplation and meditation. In all of them the theme is one and the same, and to live in breathless harmony with "that Supreme Consciousness that is the Self in me" is the highest realisation.

"*I am the revealer of the Vedā-s*" (*Vedānta Kṛt*):— Any knowledge if it were to come to any individual, the knower must know it as his conscious idea. Without Consciousness the idea striking an intellect has no existence at all *for the individual*. The very thinker is impossible without Consciousness playing on his thoughts. Since this Consciousness is my true nature, all the scientific observations made, the logical conclusions arrived at and the right efforts put forth so far in order to withdraw myself from the endless tentacles of the *Avidyā*-octopus are all rendered possible only in that dynamic light of this Great Light Principle.

When the release from *Avidyā* is complete, the realisation is full; and even in the last moments the objectless awareness 'knows' Itself, by Itself, being Itself of the nature of Pure Knowledge. This is implied in the next phrase used in the *Mantra* "*I alone am the real knower of the Vedā-s.*"

A knower of the *Vedā-s* is not mere mechanical intellect with a powerful throat that can bleat out the *Mantrā-s.* The words of the *Vedā-s* are vehicles to conduct the student into a realm of knowledge and until this awakening is experienced *Veda*-study is incomplete. Subjective meditation on the theme of the *Veda* alone is "knowing" the *Veda* and the knower of the *Veda* naturally is one who has realised the Self (*Ātma-vit*) and there his individuality would have merged to express itself as the Infinite Reality, the *Brahman*.

These two opening lines of the *Mantra* with a very little insignificant difference is met with in the *Śrīmad Bhagavad Gītā* (XV-15). There the stanza was in the mouth of Lord *Kṛṣṇa*, considered as the fullest incarnation of the Infinite, according to the *Purāṇā-s*. But here in this *Upaniṣad* it is an ordinary mortal, born into ignorance who had, through study, reflection, self-discipline and meditation, climbed over the peaks of perfection that is declaring the very same stanza. Neither the *Upaniṣad* Seer nor the author of the *Brahma Sūtrā-s* was fool enough to make the same stanza fall from the mouth of a mortal in meditation and also play upon the lips of the Divine flute-bearer of *Vṛṁdāvan*. The significance should not be over looked.

It is not the cowherd boy, *Rādhā's* beloved, the Charioteer Brother-in-law of *Arjuna*, that was talking when He said "*I am the theme, the author and the knower of the Vedā-s.*" Similarly, it was not a hunter who daily looted the pilgrims that wrote the *Rāmāyaṇa*; *Vālmīki* alone could accomplish that poetic feat. A graduate of the Calcutta University, *Narendra* could have never accomplished, what *Vivekānanda* did. The ineffectual Prince *Siddhārtha* is not *Gautama Buddha*, the Prince of Compassion.

The student, who came to the teacher is not the one who is talking in this *Mantra*; that individually was long ago dead at the frontiers of the intellect, crossing which he has become, as he humbly declares now "*the theme, the author and the knower of the Veda.*" At the transcendental moments, distinctions dissolve. Time stops. Truth alone is.............. Knowing Truth, as Truth, established in Truth; It is Pure and Uncontaminated. It is Immaculate and nothing can ever soil It.

"*For me there is neither merit nor de-merit*":—Merit (*Puṇya*) and de-merit (*Pāpa*) are all foot prints left over on the personality by the types of thoughts and actions it had entertained and committed. These *Vāsanā-s* can condition only thoughts which in their turn can enslave the individuality. But once the thoughts are transcended, *Vāsanā-s* get exploded; and what remains beyond the *Vāsanā-s* is the *Immaculate Non-dual Reality*.

"I *suffer no destruction*":—Since there is the law of conservation of matter, nothing in the world outside can ever be destroyed. This is applicable in the subtler realm of thoughts also; thoughts entertained in the past may seemingly look as if ended, but they re-live to condition the new sets of thoughts. What goes in the name of destruction is not, therefore, for the "existence" of the thing, but only for its form, quality, name, etc. These may change, and therefore, the name also may change, and with reference to the present condition we may say that the old condition is destroyed.

Since the Infinite Self has none of these changeables in It and It being the very "existence" in all things at all times, It suffers no change. The pot may break, but the very substance with which the pot is made can never die.

"*Birth*":—That which is born shall necessarily die. Birth is only for a finite material object. The new birth is only the destruction of its previous state of former condition. Since the Self has no destruction, it can never be born. It was, is and shall ever be. It is the very substratum upon which the delusory modifications such as birth, growth, decay, disease and death are taking place. The substratum is never conditioned by the super impositions. The "*serpent*' cannot give any poison to the *rope*—

the "*ghost*" cannot leave its foot prints near the *post*— the "*mirage-waters*" cannot wet the arid *sands of the desert*. The Self is never born, even at the birth of the body. It was already there to illumine that experience.

Since It is never born, from Its standpoint and observation, It has no experience of either the body or the mind, or the intellect. From the standpoint of the Waker, he is no more conscious of the new children born to the last night's dream-wife. The term birth (*Janma*) is nothing but our identification with our body, mind and intellect. Such a false identification with the non-existent world of matter is not possible for the Self; because the awakened one cannot identify himself as the father of the children born in his yesterday's dream.

न भूमिरापो न च वह्निरस्ति
न चानिलो मेऽस्ति न चाम्बरं च ।
एवं विदित्वा परमात्मरूपं
गुहाशयं निष्कलमद्वितीयम् ॥ २३ ॥

Na bhūmir-āpo na ca vahnir-asti
na cānilo me-'sti na cāmbaraṁ ca,
evam viditvā paramātma-rūpaṁ
guhāśayaṁ niṣkalam-advitīyam.

न *na* = not; भूमि: *bhūmiḥ* = earth; आप: *āpaḥ* = water; न *na* = not; च *ca* = and; वह्नि: *vahniḥ* = fire; अस्ति *asti* = is; न *na* = not; च *ca* = and; अनिल: *anilaḥ* = air; मे *me* = my; अस्ति *asti* = is; न *na* = not; च *ca* = and; अम्बरम् *ambaram* = ether, sky; च *ca* = and; एवम् *evam* = thus; विदित्वा *viditvā* = knowing; परमात्म-रूपम् *paramātma-rūpam* = the nature of the *Paramātman*, the Supreme Self; गुहा-शयम् *guhā-śayam* = staying in the cavity (of the heart); निष्कलम् *niṣkalam* = without phases; अद्वितीयम् *advitīyam* = non-dual.

समस्तसाक्षिं सदसद्विहीनं
प्रयाति शुद्धं परमात्मरूपम् ॥ २४ ॥

Samasta-sākṣiṁ sad-asad-vihīnaṁ,
prayāti śuddhaṁ paramātma-rūpam.

समस्त-साक्षिम् *samasta-sākṣim* = witness of all; सद्-असद्-विहीनम् *sad-asad-vihīnam* = without existence and non-existence; प्रयाति *prayāti* = reaches; शुद्धम् *śuddham* = pure; परमात्म-रूपम् *paramātma-rūpam* = the nature of the *Paramātman*, the Supreme Self.

23-24. *For me there is neither Earth nor Water nor Fire, nor Air, nor Ether. Thus realising the nature of the* Paramātman ...... *the one who is in the cavity of the heart, who is without parts, without a second, the Witness of all, beyond both existence and non-existence, one attains the very nature of the* Paramātman.

"For me there is neither the Earth nor Water, nor Fire nor Air nor Ether":—This statement is essential in removing a natural doubt that might rise in the rational intellect of any student. He may concede in his devotion for and his faith in his teacher that such a transcendental experience may be possible subjectively in the individual. But the objective world has an independent experience apart from the subjective experience of the individual. One may annihilate one's own mind, but thereby has not annihilated the great elements and their manifestations. What happens to them? May be this transcendental experience is only the subjective Divine Mood, lived only during the still hours of one's meditation within oneself; the gross world-of-objects will be staggeringly waiting solidly rooted in its own reality in the without.

To remove this idea, the teacher negates the very existence of the five Great Elements here. Please note that the enumeration of the five elements is from tthe grossest to the subtlest—"Earth, Water, Fire, Air and Space." The significance is quite evident. The grossest Earth, which has its own property of "smell" has also got all the properties of all the other elements,[1] and is, therefore, perceivable by all the sense organs in us. We can smell, taste, see, touch and hear the Earth Principle. The subtlest of the elements is Space with its own property "sound" and we know Space is a concept of the intellect. Thus, so long as we are identifying with our intellect and functioning through it, we cannot stand apart from the concept of Space nor can we reach a state of complete and absolute silence.[2]

One who has transcended the intellect comes to experience and live as the Self, and the five Gross Elements are transcended automatically.[3]

"*Thus having understood*" (*Viditvā*):— From the root *Vid*—to know, meaning, having thus realised in our own subjective personal experience, the nature of the Infinite Self (*Paramātma rūpam*) one attains full liberation from all his sense of limitations and the consequent thraldom of matter. The descriptive phrases that follow hereunder map out the nature of Truth and describe the altar at which we can receive intimation from the Highest.

"*Without parts, without a second*" (*Niṣkalam advitīyam*):— The Infinite cannot have parts as it is All-pervading, the limited alone can have parts. That which has parts must necessarily have a form, and all that have a form are perishable. The Imperishable and the Eternal, therefore, must be unconditioned and all pervading. If there is anything other than It, in It, then It would be limited; therefore, It must be non-dual (*Advitīyam*).

"*Witness of all*" (*Samasta Śākṣi*):— We have already described this idea,[4] that the Self, the Infinite, even when It is

1. Smell, Taste, Form, Touch and Sound.
2. Sound is the property of Space. In meditation till the last, sound is a sense disturbance that you canot avoid. Even in '*Savikalpa Samādhi*' there is sound. When the sound is transcended you have trancended your individuality.
3. *Na Kartṛvaṁ na karmāṇi lokasya srajati prabhūḥ* —Ref. *Bh. Gītā* (V-14)
4. The macrocosmic expression of the microcosmic sense organs is the five Great Elements. Read introduction to Chapter IX in Discourses on the *Gītā*.

recognised in our delusion to be acting, feeling or thinking, never, in fact, gets involved in these activities of the equipments (*prakṛti*) but ever stands apart as a disinterested observer,* lending its grace equally to all, at all times.

"*Beyond both existence and non-existence*" (*Sad-asad-vihīnam*):—These two are intellectual estimations. The presence of a thing or its absence are both the judgements of the intellect, regarding a theme of the observation in the outer world, and both these *concepts of the existence* of things or the *non-existence* of the same are known by the Consciousness of the observer.

The Consciousness that illumines the judgements of the intellect must be something other than the very judgements themselves. The ideas of existence and non-existence can describe or define the world of things in the relative field; but these terms cannot define Truth, since It is the very Knowing Principle with which we know all our experiences in the relative field. Everything perceived, felt and known in the empirical fields of life can fall under these two categories, as existence and non-existence. But the Consciousness, that illumines them is constantly beyond them—and hence the Infinite is defined in the *Upaniṣad* here as *Sad-asad-vihīnam.*

"*This great Paramātman*":—Without Parts, Non-dual Witness of all and beyond all intellectual concept of existence and non-existence—is a Truth no doubt worth realising: But where can It be realised? It is so all-pervading and seems to transcend everything known that It eludes our comprehension and It seems that It has no abode of Its own.

Here the *mantra* describes "*Truth as lying in the heart*" (*Guhāśayam*):—Just as the Government of a country is throughout the country and yet in order to contact the government we have to make a pilgrimage towards its capital, which is the seat of the Government; so too the All-pervading,

* Ibid, *Mantra*-18.

Omnipresent Self can be contacted in its seat Divine, in the very heart of the seeker.

Here the term "heart" is not the physiological heart. Here it means only the core of the personality in the very seeker. *Heart* stands for the humane virtues in man. One who develops and cultivates love, kindness, sympathy, charity, cheerfulness, peace, joy tranquillity etc., is developing his heart.

In such a harmonised bosom, protected well from the wild storms of passion, is the altar where Truth can be realised in the very temple of the body.*

Realising this great Truth one attains (*Prayāti*) the experience of Pure (*Śuddham*) State of *Paramātmā*-hood (*Paramātma-rūpam*). One attaining the *Paramātman* is something like the dreamer attaining waker-hood.

With this joyous assertion guaranteeing a cent percent success of all true and serious seeekers, the first chapter of the *Kaivalyopaniṣad* concludes.

इति प्रथम: खण्ड: ॥

Iti prathamaḥ khaṇḍaḥ.

इति *iti* = thus; प्रथम: *prathamaḥ* = first; खण्ड: *khaṇḍaḥ* = part.

End of Part I.

There is no second part as such. But at the close of this *Upaniṣad* we find two more *mantrā-s* (numbered by us as Pp-1 and Pp-2) which are again psychological encouragements (detailing attainment of fruits—*Phala prāpti*) provided for the students who even after intellectually appreciating the *Kaivalyopaniṣad*, are hesitant to live the philosophy and get the experience.

* These phrases that are used here are reminiscent of *Kaṭhopaniṣad* (I-ii-12) "*Taṁ durdarśaṁ gūḍham-anupraviṣṭam guhāhitaṁ......*"

This hesitation is generally because of the self-consciousness of one's own moral defects, or due to the memories of one's own perpetuated crimes of calculated villainy done during moments of blindening passions. Students who have hesitation in themselves must be helped to redeem themselves from such self-persecutions and hence we have here the following :

यः शतरुद्रीयमधीते सोऽग्निपूतो भवति,
सुरापानात्पूतो भवति,
ब्रह्महत्यात्पूतो भवति,
कृत्याकृत्यात्पूतो भवति,
तस्मादविमुक्तमाश्रितो भवति।
अत्याश्रमी सर्वदा सकृद्वा जपेत् ॥ (फ.प.-१)

Yaḥ śatarudrīya-madhīte so-'gnipūto bhavati,
surā-pānāt-pūto bhavati,
brahma-hatyāt-pūto bhavati,
kṛtyā-kṛtyāt-pūto bhavati,
tasmād-avimuktam-āśrito bhavati,
atyāśramī sarvadā sakṛdvā japet.

यः *yaḥ* = who; शत-रुद्रीयम् *śata-rudrīyam* = *śatarudrīya*, (see commentary); अधीते *adhīte* = studies; सः *saḥ* = he; अग्नि-पूतः *agni-pūtaḥ* = purified by fire; भवति *bhavati* = becomes; सुरा-पानात् *surā-pānāt* = from drinking wine; पूतः *pūtaḥ* = purified; भवति *bhavati* = becomes; ब्रह्म-हत्यात् *brahma-hatyāt* = from killing a *brāhmaṇa*; पूतः *pūtaḥ* = purified; भवति *bhavati* = becomes; कृत्य-अकृत्यात् *kṛtya-ckṛtyāt* = from commissions and omissions; पूतः *pūtaḥ* = purified; भवति *bhavati* = becomes; तस्मात् *tasmāt* = therefore; अविमुक्तम् *avimuktam* = one who does not leave Truth Consciousness; आश्रितः *āśritaḥ* = gains (his) refuge; भवति *bhavati* = become; अत्याश्रमी *atyāśramī* = belonging to the highest order of life; सर्वदा *sarvadā* = always; सकृत् *sakṛt* = once; वा *vā* = or; जपेत् *japet* = repeat (this text).

Pp-1. He who studies the Śatarudrīya becomes purified by fire, is purified from the sin of drinking, is purified from the sin of killing a brāhmaṇa, is purified from sin arising from all commissions and omissions. Therefore, he gains his refuge in the One who never leaves the Truth Consciousness, Śiva, the Supreme Self. One who belongs to the highest order of Life should repeat this always or at least once (a day).

"*Śata-rudrīyam*":—This is the title given to a prayer in hundred stanzas, invoking *Rudra,* which we read in *Taittirīya Saṁhitā* of the *Yajur Veda.* Here the very *Kaivalyopaniṣad* is denoted by the same divinely suggestive title so that the students may repeat the *Upaniṣad-s* with the same faith, ardent devotion and total dedication as they do in the chanting of the *Rudra Śatarudrīyam.*

Evidently the student who has reached the teacher was himself a devotee a *Śiva* (Not a '*Śaivait*') as it is evident in the body of *Upaniṣad.* To a devotee of Lord *Śiva* in the *Vedik* days the *Śata-rudrīya* stanzas are very sacred and inspiring. With the same reverence this *Upaniṣad* is to be repeated and used for chanting, is the suggestion when the *Kaivalya* is mentioned here as the *Śata-rudrīya.* Some commentators of the *Upaniṣad* elucidating the term say that this *Upaniṣad* is *Brahma Śata-rudrīyam.*

Hesitation to give up the old ways of life and the lack of confidence to take the Divine ways of living in himself are the only reasons why an ordinary enthusiast refuses to take up religion seriously. The thick coating of memories and desires in one's personality takes away one's moral fire and inspite of his self-glorification and social status, he is indeed a coward in himself with no confidence in his own goodness.

He cannot escape from the ever-accusing conscience in himself. He runs into various fields of intense activities in order to escape from himself and bleeding memories of his past crimes, mourning and wailing, weeping and screaming, accusing and impeaching .... but wherever he may go and whatever he may do, the ghost of his past crimes follows him. Nobody can escape from himself.

The slashing chords of the whip of repentence plough us from behind. The crushing weight of regrets pulls us down. The cruel forks of sorrows at the crimes perpetrated pierce us a thousand times every minute. Lacerated and bleeding the inner personality is ever in the shackles of sorrow, helplessly sobbing at the voiceless sorrows of the terrible punishments of the Conscience.

Such an individual cannot stand apart from his own *Vāsanā-s* and so long as he is panting with the fatigue of carrying this load of the past, he cannot have any taste for the higher, and even if he is given an inkling of the Great Self, he has not got the masculinity (*Puruṣatvam*) to act up to it. Against the spotless purity of the Self even his minor defects get magnified and he becomes unnerved, benumbed, and paralysed.

Such a student must be revived, replenished, reset on the right path of pursuit. It can be done only by a psychological treatment which is being given here in this *mantra*.

Fire was the altar of worship in the *Vedik* days just as today we worship *Kṛṣṇa, Rāma, Śiva* etc. Our blasphemous life in the past should naturally forge chains on our feet. Dragging them, we dare not walk upto the very sacred altar of the Lord to surrender and to prostrate. This hesitation is removed from the mind of the student when he is told that he who studies this *Brahma-Śata-Rudrīya* meaning the *Kaivalyopaniṣad*, becomes purified from all such sins. Similarly a man of sensual pursuits would be committing a thousand such immoral and amoral acts, such as drinking etc. In his vigour and thoughtless-ness he might have insulted, disobeyed, even persecuted some man of knowledge and culture, or a real *paṇḍita* (*brāhmaṇa*) or in such a thousand different ways of ommissions and commissions must have gathered to himself, a lot of distracting residual impressions called sins. They are all eliminated and totally wiped out, says the kindly *Ṛṣi*, when we repeatedly study the *Kaivalyopaniṣad*.

When once the *Vāsanā-s* are removed, as a result of that (*Tasmāt*), one comes to surrender oneself to Lord *Śiva* and starts depending upon him more and more. *Avimukta** means one who never leaves the Truth Consciousness. Thus the term *Avimukta* denotes Lord *Śiva* and it is a common epithet known very widely in the *Śāstra* literature meaning, "That one who never leaves you even though you leave him."

Mud is *Avimukta* in the pot, Consciousness Divine is *Avimukta* in the individuality in us (*Jīva*) ; the reflection has no existence apart from its object.

"*One who is in the Highest Order of Life*" (*Atyāśramī*) must repeat this stanza always or at least once a day. We should not limit the meaning of the statement to the direct import of these words. The term *Atyāśramī* was earlier used in the same *Upaniṣad* (*mantra*-5) wherein we have found it is only a mental attitude and not an actual change of the garb. Thus in that mental attitude of complete detachment from all matter envelopments, the student must be able to read the *Kaivalyopaniṣad* as often as he can (*Sarvadā*), and if this is not possible, at least he must once a day read this *Upaniṣad*.

This technique of reading the scriptures regularly has been the constant advice of the scriptural teachers to the early students in *Vedānta*. This is technically known as *Svādhyāya*.

In this *mantra* it is interesting to note that the term used for studying (*Adhīte*) is very significant. "*Dhī*" means "*buddhi*"

1. It is interesting that we have got a place in *Banāras* called *Avimukta*. The tradition, which explains the *Upaniṣad* term, is that even at the time of the Great Annihilation of the world (*Pralaya*) Lord *Śiva* and his consort would never leave the sacred spot of *Avimukta*.

the intellect; therefore, *Adhīte* etymologically means "brings the idea into the intellect." Without assimilation of an idea it is not considered that one's education is complete. Philosophical ideas are not just to be understood but are to be assimilated and lived.

अनेन ज्ञानमाप्नोति संसारार्णवनाशनम् ।
तस्मादेवं विदित्वैनं कैवल्यं फलमश्नुते
कैवल्यं फलमश्नुते इति ॥ (फ.प.-२)

Anena jñānam-āpnoti saṁsārārṇava-nāśanam,
tasmād-evaṁ viditvainaṁ kaivalyaṁ phalam-aśnute
kaivalyaṁ phalamaśnuta iti.

अनेन *anena* = by this; ज्ञानम् *jñānam* = knowledge; आप्नोति *āpnoti* = attains; संसार-अर्णवः-नाशनम् *saṁsāra-arṇavaḥ-nāśanam* = which destroys the ocean of transmigration; तस्मात् *tasmāt* = therefore; एवम् *evam* = thus; विदित्वा *viditvā* = knowing; एनम् *enam* = him; कैवल्यम् *kaivalyam* = liberation; फलम् *phalam* = fruit; अश्नुते *aśnute* = attains. कैवल्यम् फलमश्नुते इति *kaivalyam phalam-aśnute iti* = thus (one) attains the fruits of *Kaivalya.*

*Pp-2. By this one attains the knowledge that destroys the endless experience of change (repeated transmigration). Therefore, having experienced this, one attains the fruits of liberation (*Kaivalya*); indeed, one attains* Kaivalya.

"*By this*" (*Anena*) :— In the previous chapter the *Kaivalyopaniṣad* explained the three states of Consciousness and indicated that the common Principle of Reality in the waker, dreamer and deep sleeper is one and the same, which is the Self—not only of the individual but of all. On awakening into this State of Godhood, the individuality is shattered once for ever. It is interesting here to note that the Truth which was explained till now as "That" (*Tat*) is defined in this concluding stanza as "This" (*Anena*). In the language of the *Upaniṣad-s* it implied "the Truth, which was an object of intellectual appreciation only, has now become a living experience, most intimate and dear," and hence the appropriateness in using here the Pronoun "This" (*Anena*).

"*Attains the Knowledge*":—"Knowledge" (*Jñāna*) is used in *Vedānta* as the antithesis of ignorance (*Ajñāna*). The non-apprehension of Reality, creates delusory misconception (*Ajñāna*) of the ego-ruled life, and the right apprehension of the Truth (*Jñāna*) lifts away not only the sense of individuality (ego) but also all its false relationships[1] in the outer world, and the unhealthy estimation which the ego makes of things and beings around.

To the awakened one, his dream experiences of last night cannot continue. Once this Experience Divine has come to one, he fulfils his evolution[2] and crosses over the shackles of all his *Vāsānā-s*. He has, thereafter, none of the relative experiences provided by the ever-changing instruments of his crooked mind and restless intellect.

Therefore, having thus experienced this Great Self within and without one attains the "*fruits of Kaivalya*—"*Kaivalya*" in *Saṁskṛta* means "mere." *Kaivalya* is the noun form of *Kevala* and, therefore, mereliness—meaning homogeneous oneness.

We have already explained earlier that the tariff walls between the states of Consciousness are insurmountably high and the iron-curtains between them are efficiently guarded. The goods of one state are totally banned in all others; none dares smuggle across the frontiers. Thus when an individual transcends all vehicles[3] and awakes himself to the fourth-plane-of-Consciousness"[4]—there the infinite Self alone "IS." In the

---

1. Dearer than the mother, father, wife, children and wealth etc., as the *Bṛhadāraṇyaka Upaniṣad* indicates.
2. Transcends even the causal body.
3. The Gross, the Subtle and the Causal bodies.
4. The *Turīya* state of Consciousness as explained in *Svāmījī's* Discourses on *Māṇḍūkya* and *Kārikā*.

Infinite, the finite has no place at all. This experience of the One Truth (*Bhūmā*) is indicated here as the "*Kaivalya Padavī.*" Naturally, the result of *Kaivalya* is the total awakening from all delusions and delusory sense of limitations.

This last phrase is repeated twice, which is the traditional style in the *Upaniṣad-s*. It not only indicates that the *Upaniṣad* is over but also it confirms a statement which has no other arguments except the experience of the Masters.

इत्यथर्ववेदे कैवल्योपनिषत्समाप्ता ।

Ity-atharva-vede kaivalyopaniṣat-samāptā.

Here ends the *Kaivalyopaniṣad* belonging to the *Atharva Veda*.

Oṁ tat sat

Alphabetical Index to *Ślokā-s*

Note : There is no second part or chapter to the *Kaivalya Upaniṣad* although at the close, we find one more *mantra* split into two parts enunciating its greatness (*māhātmyam*) and attainment of fruits (*Phala-prāpti*) as a result of its regular study. Some of the publications have numbered this *mantra* as 25. In order to distinguish in the Alphabetical Index, we have numbered these as Pp-1 and Pp-2 where 'Pp' stands for *Phala-prāpti*—-Ed.